Thinking about Human Life and Society

人間生活と社会福祉を読み解く新たな視点

編著者

茨木正志郎 （Seishirou Ibaraki）
Sam Haugh （サム・ホー）
中野陽子 （Yoko Nakano）
西村浩子 （Hiroko Nishimura）
小林亮哉 （Ryoya Kobayashi）

Thinking about Human Life and Society
人間生活と社会福祉を読み解く新たな視点

Download Audio
音声ファイル
無料 DL
のご案内

このテキストの音声を無料で視聴（ストリーミング）・ダウンロードできます。自習用音声としてご活用ください。
以下のサイトにアクセスしてテキスト番号で検索してください。

https://nanun-do.com　テキスト番号［**512173**］

※ 無線 LAN（WiFi）に接続してのご利用を推奨いたします。

※ 音声ダウンロードは Zip ファイルでの提供になります。
お使いの機器によっては別途ソフトウェア（アプリケーション）の導入が必要となります。

Thinking about Human Life and Society 音声ダウンロードページは左記の QR コードからもご利用になれます。

Read by

Shizuka Anderson
Ryan Drees

まえがき

現代の日本には、所得格差や少子高齢化、医療、保健、保育、健康などの様々な社会問題があり、これらの諸問題にどのように適切に対応していくかということが課題となっております。またそれに伴い、これらの分野における話題や情報が急速に増えており、私たち一人ひとりが関連する分野の情報について関心を持ち理解を深めることが大切だといえるでしょう。
このテキストは、社会の中で問題を抱えている人たちがより幸せに暮らすために取り組んでいる各分野の研究者たちの実践について比較的平易な英語で紹介しています。全体は１５課で構成され、各課は、福祉に関する英文を軸に、以下の５つのセクションが有機的に配置され、語彙の増強、読解力の向上、文法の復習、リスニング・ライティング力の向上をねらいとしています。

⋙ **Warm-up Activities:** 本文の内容に関連した写真や各課のトピックに関する質問を通して学習者の興味を喚起し、新出語句や重要語句について確認します。

⋙ **Reading Activities:** 500 ～ 600 語程度のテキストを読み、Comprehension Check で設問に答えながら内容を深めます。さらに Summary で本文の内容を確認します。

⋙ **Writing Activities:** 本文に出てきた文法や構文を利用した並べ替えや英作文のアクティビティを通じ、英語での表現力を養います。

⋙ **Listening Activities:** 本文に出てきた、語彙・語句などの発音を確認し、本文の内容に関する穴埋め問題やディクテーションを通じ、意味を効率よく聞き取る練習をします。

⋙ **Another Challenge:** 本文の内容について自分の意見を述べることで、自律的・発展的学習へとつなげます。

本書の５つの特徴

１．教材や練習問題が易しいものから高いものに配置してあり、徐々に流暢さを高めることができるように構成されています。

２．言語使用者としての自立性を高めるため、練習問題の内容が徐々に学習者中心の活動に移行するように構成されています。

３．リーディングの教科書ではありますが、リスニング、ライティング、スピーキングの技能を使うタスクを含めることで多角的に学習内容を身につけられるように配慮しています。

４．福祉に関するトピックを広い領域に渡って専門家が書いています。

５．社会福祉に関連した語彙を学べるように配慮してあります。

本書は巻末に記載されている方々の協力によって作成されました。心より御礼を申し上げます。学生の皆さんが、各ユニットの英文を通して英語力を養い、現代の諸問題について関心と理解を深め、それぞれの問題について自ら積極的に考え学んでいく姿勢を身に着けていってほしいと願っています。

編著者

CONTENTS

目次

Unit 1 Health and Social Welfare

健康と社会福祉

≫ Warm-up Activities

A 下記の質問について話し合ってみましょう。

1. What do you think “health” means?
2. Do you know how many people die from cancer in Japan each year?
3. What kind of support do you think we can provide for a family member who is ill?

B 下記の語句に該当する日本語を右から選び、その記号を（　）に書き入れましょう。

1. (　　) well-being
2. (　　) patient
3. (　　) cancer
4. (　　) treatment
5. (　　) physical
6. (　　) anxiety
7. (　　) medical
8. (　　) mental

(a) 身体的な
(b) 癌
(c) 精神的な
(d) 幸福
(e) 医学の
(f) 不安、心配
(g) 患者
(h) 治療

C Bに出てきた語句を（　　）に入れて文を完成させてください。必要な場合は形を変えてください。

1. (　　　　　　　　) activity can help reduce (　　　　　　　　) and depression.

2. He always looks after his brother's emotional (   ).
3. The (   ) was kept alive by the artificial heart for almost five months.
4. Cigarette smoking multiplies the risk of (   ).
5. The more (   ) science advances, the more expensive (   ) are becoming.

Health and Social Welfare

How would you respond if you were asked to define health? Many people probably believe that being healthy means not getting sick or ill. The Charter of the World Health Organization[1] signed in 1946 and brought into force in 1948 considered people's health to be fundamental to the attainment of peace and security, and declares that "Health is a state of complete physical, mental and social well-being and not merely the absence of disease or infirmity." From this perspective, when approaching various health problems, holistic practices are required not only for the body but also for the human mind and social environment.

1. ______________ 定義する
2. ______________ 基本的な
3. ______________ 達成
4. ______________ 宣言する
5. ______________ 病弱
6. ______________ 観点
7. ______________ 全体的な

A survey by the Ministry of Health, Labour and Welfare conducted in 2014 made it clear that there is an extremely meaningful relationship between the state of one's health and one's feeling of happiness. Health is important for the happiness of all people, and social welfare uses specific methods to achieve it. Therefore, there is a strong affinity between health and social welfare, and while Japan has a robust social support system relative to other developed nations, there are still areas that require attention.

8. ______________ 有意義な
9. ______________ 特定の
10. ______________ 関連性
11. ______________ 強靭な

For example, in recent years, the number of elderly people living with some kind of disease has been on the increase, which causes troubling mental and social issues, such as solitude and isolation. Therefore, social support is essential to the health of the elderly.

12. ______________ 孤独
13. ______________ 孤立

Also, support such as adjustments in workplace environments is needed for the rising number of people suffering from mental health problems caused by chronic social stress from daily life. Such health-related problems are closely linked to and have a major impact on all our daily lives.

14. ________________ 慢性的

Health-related issues are a particular threat to our well-being due to the stress they cause. For example, while more and more cancer patients are recovering thanks to the advances in medical science, people still generally believe that cancer is a recurring, metastatic, incurable disease. For this reason, cancer patients and their families often feel uncertainty, anxiety, and fear about the future. In addition, patients who have to quit their jobs to receive medical treatment will also experience financial anxiety.

15. ________________ 脅威

16. ________________ 再発する

17. ________________ 転移する

18. ________________ 治らない

19. ________________ 不確実性

Another problem with cancer is that the family of a cancer patient is considered a "secondary patient," and they are expected to fulfill the role of a caregiver. This can have a major impact on the family's lifestyle. For example, the burden of taking on new roles, such as housework and childcare, causes friction within the family and leads to the deterioration of family relationships. Adding to that, family members of cancer patients who must provide end-of-life care may have to make serious decisions on whether to provide life-prolonging treatments[2] or to allow them to die with dignity[3]. Thus, health-related problems involve not only physical treatment for the patient, but also the need for livelihood support for the patient's family.

20. ________________ 二次的な

21. ________________ を果たす

22. ________________ 看護者

23. ________________ 負荷

24. ________________ 不和

25. ________________ 悪化

In summary, health and social welfare are closely interrelated, and both must take into account emotional and social issues. As a result, social welfare programs in Japan aim to enhance human well-being and contribute to health by being engaged in solving life problems.

26. ____________ 高める

(518 words)

✦ **Notes/ 注**

1. The Charter of the World Health Organization: 世界保健機関憲章
2. life-prolonging treatment: 延命治療
3. die with dignity: 尊厳のある死

⋙ Comprehension Check

D 内容に関する文を完成させるために、最も適切なものを選んでください。

1. What is The Charter of the World Health Organization's position on health?

A. It is important to the attainment of peace and security.

B. It is fundamental not to be sick or ill, but it is irrelevant whether one feels mental well-being or not.

C. It is essential to address health issues, including the body, human mind, and social environment, holistically.

D. It is crucial to approach various health problems.

2. Which of the following has NOT been revealed by the survey conducted by the Ministry of Health, Labour and Welfare?

A. There is an extremely meaningful relationship between the state of one's health and one's feeling of happiness.

B. There is a strong affinity between health and social welfare.

C. Japan has a robust social support system relative to other developed nations.

D. Thanks to social welfare, which uses special methods to achieve the happiness of all people, there are few areas that require attention.

3. What causes troubling mental and social issues, such as solitude and isolation?

A. The rising number of elderly people with some kind of disease

B. The rising number of people suffering from mental health problems

C. Adjustments in workplace environments

D. Chronic social stress from daily life

4. What do many people misunderstand about cancer?

A. Cancer is a threat to our well-being.

B. More and more cancer patients are recovering thanks to advances in medical science.

C. Cancer is a recurring, metastatic, incurable disease.

D. Cancer patients feel uncertainty, anxiety, and fear about the future.

5. What is caused by the burden of taking on new roles, such as housework and childcare?

A. The family of a cancer patient is considered a “secondary patient.”

B. The family of a cancer patient is expected to fulfill the role of caregiver.

C. The family of a cancer patient must provide end-of-life care.

D. The family relationships of a cancer patient’s family get worse.

≫ Summary

E (　)にあてはまる語句を語群から選んで入れて、本文の要約を完成させてください。

Health is important for the (**1.**　) of all people, and social welfare uses (**2.**　) methods to achieve it. Therefore, there is a strong (**3.**　) between health and social welfare. Social support, such as (**4.**　) in workplace environments, is needed for the rising number of people (**5.**　) from mental health problems. Health-related issues are a particular (**6.**　) to our well-being due to the stress they cause. In addition, patients who have to quit their jobs to (**7.**　) medical treatment will also experience financial (**8.**　). Thus, health-related problems involve not only physical treatment for the patient, but also the need for livelihood support for the patient’s family. As a result, social welfare programs in Japan aim to (**9.**　) human well-being and (**10.**　) to health by being engaged in solving life problems.

✦ 語群

a. receive	b. suffering	c. contribute	d. affinity	e. specific
f. happiness	g. enhance	h. adjustments	i. anxiety	j. threat

⋙ Writing Activities < 品詞 part of speech>

F 次の英文中の下線部には英単語が入ります。[　　] の単語を適切な品詞に変え、日本語訳を参考にして、文を完成させましょう。

1. 我々は難しいけれども達成可能な目標を設定するべきだ。

   We should set challenging but ____________ goals. **[attain]**

2. 他の店と比べると、この店は値段が比較的安い。

   Compared to other stores, prices are ____________ low at the store. **[relative]**

3. 私は娘のことが非常に心配だ。

   I am very ____________ about my daughter. **[anxiety]**

G 日本語の意味になるように、(　　) 内の語句を並び替えましょう。

1. 彼女は怪我から完全に回復した。

   She (her injuries / has / from / fully recovered).

   ____

2. その薬は癌の治療に効く。

   The (effective / of cancer / medicine / in / is / the treatment).

   ____

3. 我々は異なる観点からその問題に取り組まなければならない。

   We (the problem / have to / perspective / from / approach / a different).

   ____

4. 彼女の不注意な運転で父親に大きな心配をかけた。

   Her (great anxiety / caused / driving / careless / her father).

   ____

5. 彼らは彼女が無実だということを明らかにしなければならない。

   They (innocent / have to / she is / make / that / clear / it).

   ____

≫ Listening Activity 03

H Dictation ≫ Write what you hear.

1. In order to solve various health problems, holistic approaches are needed ____ __________.

2. ____________ other developed nations, Japan __________________ ____ that need to be resolved.

3. More people ____ ________________________, such as adjustments to their workplace environments.

4. Social welfare programs in Japan ___________________________ ____ by giving assistance in tackling life's difficulties.

≫ Another Challenge

I 職場環境とメンタルヘルスについて調べてみましょう。

Unit 2 Care Workers from Overseas
外国人介護労働者

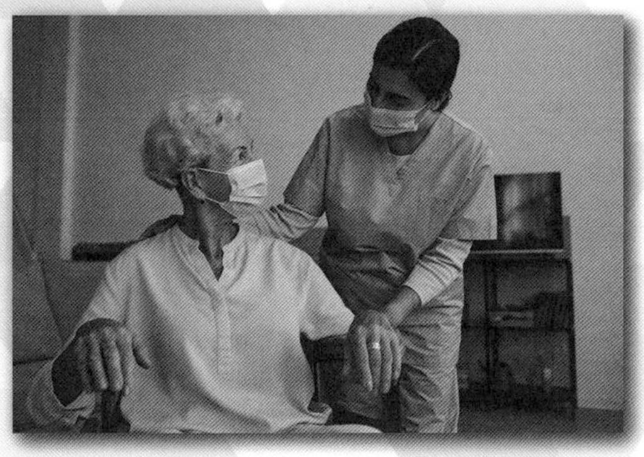

≫ Warm-up Activities

A 下記の質問について話し合ってみましょう。

1.What is the woman in the photograph above doing?
2. Where do you frequently see foreigners working in daily life?
3. What do you know about the current situation and issues of foreign workers in Japan?

B 下記の語句に該当する日本語を右から選び、その記号を（　）に書き入れましょう。

1. (　　) accelerate
2. (　　) estimate
3. (　　) candidate
4. (　　) certified
5. (　　) facility
6. (　　) qualification
7. (　　) comparable
8. (　　) acquisition

(a) 候補者
(b) 同等の
(c) 試算
(d) 資格
(e) 獲得
(f) 加速する
(g) 施設
(h) 保証された

C Bに出てきた語句を（　）に入れて文を完成させてください。必要な場合は形を変えてください。

1. Exposure to the sun is said to (　　　　　　　　) the development of skin cancer.
2. Basic education (　　　　　　　　) are those such as kindergarten and elementary schools.

3. The consumption tax in Japan is (　　　　　　　　) to the value-added tax in European countries.

4. You have to acquire a (　　　　　　　　) to work as a long-term caregiver.

5. The (　　　　　　　　) for the number of peple who died of infection from the Spanish flu between 1918 and 1921 was at least 17 million.

Foreign Care Workers in Elderly Care in Japan 04

For some time now, Japan has seen a steady decrease in fertility rate, and a gradual increase in the percentage of the population that are senior citizens. Indeed, in 2020, the aging population with people over the age of 65 exceeded 28%. As a result, the labor market has suffered a serious labor shortage, the acceptance of foreign workers has accelerated, and the number of foreign workers has reached about 1.72 million. In particular, with the number of elderly people requiring nursing care increasing to nearly 7 million, the labor shortage in elderly care is a serious problem. According to estimates by the Ministry of Health, Labour and Welfare[1], the number of care workers[2] Japan would need will be approximately 2,450,000 in 2025, but the number of care workers nationwide is currently about 2,000,000, which would be a shortage of about 380,000 in the future at the current pace that caregiver numbers are increasing. This is one of the biggest problems in an aging society with a declining birth rate.

1. ________________ 出生率
2. ________________ 人手不足
3. ________________ 加速した
4. ________________ 介護
5. ________________ 試算
6. ________________ 老齢化社会

The discussion about accepting foreign workers has been ongoing for more than a decade. Since 2008, the Indonesian and Filipino candidates who came under the Economic Partnership Agreement (EPA)[3] as certified care workers have been working in care facilities in Japan, and since 2012, Vietnamese candidates have also been coming to Japan. From 2008 to 2020, the total number of EPA candidates who arrived was only 5,491.

7. ________________ 継続中
8. ________________ 候補者
9. ________________ 認定された
10. ________________ 施設

However, in 2018, the Japanese government revised the Immigration Control and Refugee Recognition Act[4] and the Technical Intern Training Act[5] as a strategy to address the labor shortage due to the population decline. These revisions introduced a system that makes it easier for foreigners to enter the country on the condition that they work in a job such as long-term care[6], construction, manufacturing, or agriculture. As a result, it is expected that the employment of foreigners will rapidly increase in long-term care facilities.

11. ________________ 戦略
12. ________________ 取組む
13. ________________________ という条件で

So, how do people in long-term care facilities feel about this situation? For the most part, foreign care workers are polite, serious, and warmly involved with the elderly, so they are highly valued by colleagues, the elderly, and their families. On the other hand, care workers are required to have a high level of communicative ability, and foreign care workers often have insufficient Japanese conversation and literacy skills. Moreover, there are concerns about cultural differences, values, and lifestyles between Japanese and foreigners.

14. ________________ 関わって
15. ________________ 不十分な
16. ________________ 読み書き

Unfortunately, there are some long-term care providers who are willing to hire foreign care workers for low wages. They may not only violate the human rights of care workers and decrease their job satisfaction, but also lower the quality of care and society's approval in Japan, which may lead to deterioration in the quality of life of elderly patients. In order to prevent such problems, it is necessary to establish strict guidelines for hiring foreign care workers and an appropriate monitoring system for long-term care providers. In addition to improving working conditions to those comparable to that of Japanese, it is also necessary to provide

17. ________________ 評価
18. ________________ 悪化
19. ________________ 適切な
20. ________________ 監視
21. ________________ 同等の

foreign care workers with generous support for Japanese language education in the workplace and the acquisition of qualifications related to long-term care.

22. ______________ 取得
23. ______________ 資格

No doubt, some foreign care workers will return to their countries after a few years, but others want to get married, have children, have a family, and settle in Japan more permanently. How can we be more accepting of foreign workers? It is time for us to discuss how to accept them as residents, not just as temporary workers, in our communities.

24. ______________ 恒久的に

(591 words)

✦ **Notes/ 注**

1. The Ministry of Health, Labour and Welfare: 厚生労働省
2. care workers: 介護労働者
3. Economic Partnership Agreement (EPA): 経済連携協定
4. Immigration Control and Refugee Recognition Act: 入国管理法
5. Technical Intern Training Act: 技能実習法
6. long-term care: 高齢者介護

≫ Comprehension Check

D 内容に関する文を完成させるために、最も適切なものを選んでください。

1. According to the passage, in 2020 ______.

A. less than 28% of Japan's elderly population has exceeded 65 years

B. about 1.72 million foreign workers were required in Japan

C. more than one and a half million foreigners were working in Japan

D. Japan needed 2,450,000 care workers nationwide

2. From 2008 to 2020, ______.

A. 5,491 Indonesian and Filipino candidates for certified care workers came to Japan

B. Japan made several revisions in the Immigration Control and the Refugee Recognition Act

C. the employment of foreign care workers increased rapidly

D. foreign candidates for certified care workers were from Indonesia, the Philippines and Vietnam

3. Long-term care work in Japan ______.

A. is repetitive, unskilled labor and does not require special knowledge

B. is unskilled labor, but it requires some level of communication ability

C. requires a high level of Japanese proficiency

D. had better be done by Japanese workers

4. Some foreign care workers are hired for low wages because ______.

A. they have better working conditions than those for Japanese workers

B. they are provided with language training and cultural education in the workplace

C. no appropriate systems to monitor long-term care providers have been established

D. they do not violate the human rights and life quality of care receivers

5. The author suggests that ______.

A. we should discuss the conditions for accepting foreigners as permanent residents

B. it is time to accept foreign workers as permanent residents

C. foreign workers should be accepted if they follow the Japanese lifestyle

D. foreign workers should return to their countries after a certain period of time

≫ Summary

E (　　) にあてはまる語句を語群から選んで入れて、本文の要約を完成させてください。

Japan has become an (1.　　) society with a low (2.　　) rate which in turn causes serious labor (3.　　). In particular, as the number of elderly people (4.　　) long-term care increases, the need to accept (5.　　) care workers has been increasing. The Japanese government has (6.　　) its laws to accept foreigners as long-term care workers, but some care (7.　　) are willing to hire them at low wages, which results in (8.　　) the human rights of the foreigners and (9.　　) the QOL of the care receivers. We should now (10.　　) the possibility of (11.　　) necessary support to foreign care workers and accepting them as (12.　　) residents.

✦ **語群**

a. aging	b.discuss	c. fertility	d. foreign	e. permanent
f. requiring	g. revised	h. providers	i. providing	j. shortages
k. violating	l. worsening			

≫ Writing Activities < 不定詞 infinitive>

F 日本語の意味になるように、(　　) 内の語句を並べ替えましょう。

1. 言うまでもないが、留学で良い結果を出すためには強い意志とある程度の語学力が求められる。
   Needless to say, both strong motivation and a certain level of (are / abroad / language skill / to be / required / studying / successful in).

   ____

2. 炎が迫ってきたので住人は建物から避難した。
   The (approaching / evacuate / fire / made / residents / the) the building.

   ____

G 日本語の意味になるように英文を完成させましょう。

1. 幸い道幅は広かったので私の車は通り抜けられた。
   Fortunately the road was (　　　　　　　　　　).
2. 風邪をひかないようにセーターを着なさい。
   Put a sweater on (　　　　　　　　　　) cold.

3. 無能なコーチは生徒に水を飲むなと命じた。

The incompetent coach ordered the students (   ) water.

⋙ Listing Activity 05

H Dictation ⋙ Write what you hear.

1. In 2020, the number of technical intern trainees was ______________ ______________________________________.

2. ____ ________________.

3. It seems that ____ ____ ________________ living human beings.

4. The government is trying to accept foreign ____________________ ____ ____ as permanent residents.

⋙ Another Challenge

I 日本が外国人労働者の定住を受け入れた場合に想定される利点と負荷について調べてみましょう。

Unit 3 Critical Knowledge

批判知

⋙ Warm-up Activities

A 下記の質問について話し合ってみましょう。

1. What do you think the woman and the girl in the photograph are doing?
2. Do you discuss political or economic issues with your family and friends? Why or why not?
3. What do you think of when you hear the term “critical thinking”?

B 下記の語句に該当する日本語を右から選び、その記号を（　）に書き入れましょう。

1. (　　) critical
2. (　　) disadvantaged
3. (　　) impose
4. (　　) cxplore
5. (　　) engage in
6. (　　) avoidance
7. (　　) perspective
8. (　　) restriction

(a) 見方、視点
(b) 課す、負わす
(c) 参加する
(d) 不利な、不自由な
(e) 避けること
(f) 制限、制約
(g) 探る、模索する
(h) 批判的な

C Bに出てきた語句を（　）に入れて文を完成させてください。必要な場合は形を変えてください。

1. During the pandemic, governments have (　　　　　　　　　　) various restrictions on individuals and businesses.
2. Students are expected to actively (　　　　　　　　　　) class activities.

3. We need to be open to different ( ), especially when we try to create something new.
4. Career seminars provide people with opportunities to ( ) their career options.
5. ( ) thinking is a process of making logical judgements without prejudice.

Young People and Critical Thinking 06

It seems to be a worldwide custom that older generations pass on to younger generations their critical views on the current state of politics and economics. However, children, young people, and adults in Japan are severely disadvantaged when it comes to forming views about society and politics in contrast to other countries. TV personality Haruka Christine from Switzerland described the situation as follows, "Japan has no political discourse despite being an everyday occurrence." If you visit some countries in Asia and Europe, you will notice that the memories of war and political discussions are commonplace among citizens, even among children and young people. For instance, let me describe an episode when I visited a special needs school in Germany in March, 2012.

Four children between the ages of 10 to 15 were provided with the opportunity to ask me questions about Japan by their principal. The principal asked the children, "We have guests from as far away as Japan. Do you have any questions about Japan?" I wondered what they would ask me. I was a little nervous, wondering if they would ask me about Japanese animation or artists. I was prepared to answer and waited for the children to ask their questions.

Then a young girl named Jessica gently raised her hand and asked in a quiet voice, "... What is going on in Fukushima?" The mention of that

1. ______________________
批判的な見方
2. ______________________
現状
3. ______________________
不利な、不自由な
4. ______________________
～とは対照的に
5. ______________________
会話、談話
6. ______________________
日常の出来事
7. ______________________
当たり前の
8. ______________________
特別支援学校

place froze me in my tracks. I wondered why the girl was asking about Fukushima, a place where we Japanese were feeling pain. She had been very troubled by the images of Fukushima that she saw during a TV special about the Great East Japan Earthquake on March 11th. The school had been discussing Fukushima as a topic to help the children understand the situation more clearly and calm down. It was also an important topic discussed in their homes. The principal casually said, "This is what every school in Germany does. Every child is interested in Fukushima."

9. ________ その場で

10. ________ 何気なく

After World War II, two educational laws were enacted in Japan that imposed restrictions on political activities under the premise of political neutrality. Political debates are actually possible, but in schools, teachers and children shy away from them. Furthermore, since Japan's period of high economic growth, Japanese youth culture has become centered on consumption, and as a result, they have moved away from free discussions which children and young people in other countries normally engage in.

11. ________ 法律化する

12. ________ 制限

13. ________ ～という前提に基づいて

14. ________ 中立性

15. ________ ～するのを避ける

16. ________ 消費

In Japan, there is an avoidance of political and economic discussions in daily life, which differs greatly from Germany. In Japan, younger people who are neither for nor against nuclear power are becoming more and more prominent, but it seems that Jessica, who lives in Germany, is not a bystander. It is not only peace studies that German schools have been involved in. They are also providing in-depth education about economic and environmental problems which are included as a subject like any other. Furthermore, families and media outlets in Germany do not stop discussions about the state of society. This is why Jessica used this opportunity to ask her question.

17. ________ 避けること

18. ________ 顕著な

19. ________ 傍観者

20. ________ 平和学習

21. ________ 報道機関

This kind of critical thinking is an integral part of a democratic society, because society will be renewed by analyzing the current situation from various perspectives and exploring new possibilities. It seems very important for the future for students to develop appropriate critical thinking skills in school. Hopefully, their critical views of politics, economics, and society will be passed on to the next generation when they become adults. (582 words)

22. ____________ 批判知
23. ____________ 不可欠な
24. ____________ 見方、視点
25. ____________ 適切な

⋙ Comprehension Check

D 内容に関する文を完成させるために、最も適切なものを選んでください。

1. In contrast to other countries, people in Japan ______.

A. often discuss political, economic, and social issues in daily life
B. rarely discuss political, economic and social issues in daily life
C. have many opportunities to discuss political issues in school
D. do not have any opportunities to discuss political issues in homes at all

2. At a school in Germany, a young girl asked the author about ______.

A. Japan's nuclear accident
B. Japanese animation
C. Japanese artists
D. Japan's economic situation

3. In Japan, political debates are often avoided in school because ______.

A. Japanese schools do not provide peace studies
B. people in Japan are neither for nor against nuclear power
C. teachers don't know how to provide in-depth education about politics
D. educational laws imposed restrictions on political activities

4. Jessica is not a bystander because ______.

A. she has become interested in discussing social issues
B. she doesn't stop asking questions
C. she has become interested in Japanese youth culture
D. she is strongly against nuclear power

5. The author thinks it is important to allow Japanese children to discuss freely in school in order for them ______.

A. to impose restrictions on political debates

B. to pass on Japanese youth culture to the next generation

C. to engage in political activities as much as possible

D. to develop appropriate critical thinking skills

≫ Summary

E (　) にあてはまる語句を語群から選んで入れて、本文の要約を完成させてください。

It is common around the world that older generations pass on their critical (1.　　) on politics and economics to younger generations. However, people in Japan are severely (2.　　) when it comes to (3.　　) views about society and politics. When the author visited a school in Germany, a girl asked her a question about the situation in Fukushima. The author learned that children in Germany were discussing the nuclear disaster in Fukushima in their schools and homes. In Japan, teachers and students do not often discuss politics since educational laws imposed (4.　　) on political activities. There is also an (5.　　) of political and economic discussions in daily life. However, critical thinking is an (6.　　) part of a (7.　　) society. It is very important to allow Japanese children to freely discuss ideas in school in order for them to (8.　　) appropriate critical thinking skills.

✦ **語群**

a. integral	b. perspectives	c. developing	d. democratic
e. develop	f. restrictions	g. disadvantaged	h. avoidance

⋙ Writing Activities < 副詞 adverb>

F 日本語の意味になるように、(　　) 内の語句を並び替えましょう。

1. 子どもは学校で自由に考えを述べることを許されるべきだ。
   (freely / to / be / should / allowed / children) discuss ideas in school.

   ____

2. 政府の新しい政策はメディアに厳しく批判された。
   The government's new policy (severely / media / by / criticized / the / was).

   ____

3. そのセミナーは参加者が人工知能をより深く理解するのに役立つだろう。
   The seminar will help participants (more / understand / to / artificial intelligence / deeply).

   ____

G 次の２つの英文の (　　) には単語が入ります。[　　] 内の単語を適切な品詞に変え、日本語訳を参考にして、文を完成させましょう。

1. I usually dress (　　　　　) **[casual]**, but I have to dress (　　　　　) **[formal]** today to attend a party.
   いつもはカジュアルな服装ですが、今日はフォーマルな服装でパーティーに参加しなければなりません。

2. The nurse (　　　　　　) **[gentle]** touched a patient on the hand to take her pulse.
   看護師が患者さんの手にそっと触れて、脈を測っています。

≫ Listening Activity 07

H Dictation ≫ Write what you hear.

1. However, children, young people, and adults in Japan are ______ ____________________________________ about society and politics, in contrast to other countries.

2. After World War II, ____________________________________ __________________ on political activities under the premise of political neutrality.

3. In Japan, ____________________________________ in daily life, which differs greatly from Germany.

4. __________________________ of a democratic society.

≫ Another Challenge

I 批判知を育むために必要なことについて話し合ってみましょう。

Unit 4

Child Poverty

日本の子どもの貧困

⋙ Warm-up Activities

A 下記の質問について話し合ってみましょう。

1. Have you ever heard of “median equivalized disposable income”?
2. Do you think Japan is a wealthy country?
3. Do you know how many children are living under the poverty line?

B 下記の語句に該当する日本語を右から選び、その記号を（　）に書き入れましょう。

1. (　　) exacerbate	(a) 排除
2. (　　) eventually	(b) 悪化させる
3. (　　) absolute	(c) 重要度
4. (　　) threshold	(d) 入り口
5. (　　) compulsory	(e) 結局
6. (　　) exclusion	(f) 緩和する
7. (　　) alleviate	(g) 義務的な
8. (　　) priority	(h) 絶対的な

C Bに出てきた語句を（　　）に入れて文を完成させてください。必要な場合は形を変えてください。

1. That new medicine couldn’t cure the illness completely, but it could (　　　　　　　　) it somewhat.
2. Inflation and rising energy costs are (　　　　　　　　) the economy of this country.

3. The scientist couldn't find a suitable material for the new machine, but after several trials, he (   ) found it.
4. The invention of the Internet took us to the (   ) of a new era.
5. It is (   ) in Japan to wear a seat belt when you drive a car.

Child Poverty in Japan 08

There is a widespread belief that Japan is economically rich, but in recent years the number of children suffering from poverty has increased. It causes disparities in opportunities for children, such as in education, arts, travel and other cultural and social experiences, which eventually affects their future. Child poverty in Japan, therefore, requires our immediate attention.

1. ________________ 格差
2. ________________ 即座の、即時の

According to Professor Yuma Konishi's study in 2016, problems resulting from financial distress are as follows: (1) inadequate housing, diet, and clothing, (2) health and developmental effects, (3) parental labor problems and stress, (4) child abuse and neglect, (5) lack of cultural resources, (6) low academic ability, (7) lack of various experiences, (8) low self-esteem, (9) isolation and exclusion. Additionally, these multiple factors interact, which can exacerbate the difficult conditions children face in their lives.

3. ________________ 苦悩、貧苦
4. ________________ 自己肯定感

There are two main types of poverty: absolute poverty and relative poverty. Absolute poverty is a condition in which maintaining a minimum requirement for survival is difficult. Relative poverty is living below the average socio-economic level in a country. It is defined as the point where a household's income is less than half of the median equivalized disposable income[1] of the country. This standard is called the poverty line. According to a survey conducted by the Ministry of Health, Labour and Welfare[2] based on the Organization for

5. ________________ 相対的な
6. ________________ 社会経済的な
7. ________________ 中間の
8. ________________ 可処分所得（手取り）

Economic Co-operation and Development (OECD)[3] standards, the poverty threshold in 2018 was 1.24 million yen, and the poverty rate for children was 14%. Specifically, one in seven children in Japan is living in relative poverty. In the case of single-mother households, about 50% of children are in this situation.

To resolve the child poverty problem in Japan, the government passed the Act on Promotion of Policy on Poverty among Children in 2014. The government is currently working on four priority measures. One of the measures is to improve the support system, mainly for educational support, such as guaranteeing access to a quality education during the compulsory education period, working to prevent high school dropouts, and providing support for them. In addition, the government is establishing a continuous support system for women who face difficulties any time from pregnancy through to childbirth. Secondly, self-reliance support for parents in low-income families is also provided. Another measure is employment support for parents. In particular, for single-parent families, the government of Japan is providing opportunities for obtaining qualifications, re-education, and short-stay childcare services. The fourth measure is financial support, which should be seriously addressed as a public responsibility in terms of a social security issue in Japan. However, the public expenses to assist children and the child-rearing generation have not been sufficient compared to those in other developed countries. This concern must be addressed from this point on.

Japan's measures against child poverty have just begun, and while government programs have been in operation for several years, they are not sufficient. In response to this situation, many citizen groups provide direct support to families

9. ______________ 所帯

10. ______________ 法令

11. ______________ 保証する

12. ______________ 中退者

13. ______________ 自立

14. ______________ 取り組む、扱う

15. ______________ ～と比較して

to help alleviate the complex problems they face raising their children. For example, learning and dietary support are widely offered all over the country. Private scholarships are also increasing. But, at the same time, there is insufficient understanding about child poverty in Japan, which is unfortunate. Therefore, it is important to raise awareness in order to enhance public support.

(547 words)

16. ______________________
緩和する、軽くする

17. ______________________
飲食（物）の

✦ **Notes / 注**

1. equivalized disposable income: 等価可処分所得（世帯の可処分所得（いわゆる手取り）を世帯の人数の平方根で割ったもの）
2. Ministry of Health, Labour and Welfare: 厚生労働省
3. the Organization for Economic Co-operation and Development (OECD): 経済協力開発機構

⋙ Comprehension Check

D 内容に関する文を完成させるために、最も適切なものを選んでください。

1. What is the main purpose of this article?

A. To show that there are many poor children in Japan

B. To show that the government is not working hard to improve child poverty in Japan

C. To raise awareness about child poverty in order to improve the situation

D. To ask for donations

2. There are two types of poverty. What are they?

A. Absolute poverty and relative poverty

B. Poverty line and socio-economic level

C. Inadequate housing and inadequate diet

D. Lack of various experiences and lack of cultural resources

3. Which of the following is NOT true about relative poverty?

A. It is a condition in which maintaining a minimum requirement for survival is difficult.

B. The poverty threshold in 2018 was an annual income below 1.24 million yen.

C. The poverty rate for children was 14% in 2018.

D. It is living below the average socio-economic level in a country.

4. Which of the following is included in the Act on Promotion of Policy on Poverty among Children in 2014?

A. To support inadequate housing

B. Employment support for parents

C. To prevent child abuse and neglect

D. To prevent isolation and exclusion

5. Who is making up for the shortcomings of inadequate government support programs?

A. The Organization for Economic Co-operation and Development (OECD)

B. The Ministry of Health, Labor and Welfare

C. Many citizen groups

D. Nobody

≫ Summary

E (　　)にあてはまる語句を語群から選んで入れて、本文の要約を完成させてください。

Japan is said to be (1.　　), but recently the number of children suffering from (2.　　) has increased. This situation causes (3.　　) in opportunities of children and eventually will affect their future. According to a survey conducted by the government, (4.　　) children is living under the poverty line. In the case of single-mother households, about (5.　　) of children are under this line. The government has begun to take action to solve this situation and has passed the Act on Promotion of Policy on Poverty among Children in 2014. However, public support has just begun and is not sufficient. Government measures to solve this problem have been (6.　　) compared to other (7.　　). In response to this situation, many citizen groups have begun to provide various kinds of support, but they are not sufficient. We need to raise (8.　　) about this problem in order to (9.　　) public support.

✦ **語群**

a. poverty　b. one in seven　c. scarce　d. improve　e. 50%

f. awareness　g. developed countries　h. disparity　i. economically rich

≫ Writing Activities < 前置詞 preposition>

F 英文 1 ～ 7 の空所に、前置詞 in, at, for, over, off, on, up から適切なものを選び文を完成させましょう。

1. The Internet has spread all ________ the world ________ great speed.
2. We were caught ________ a huge traffic jam ________ the way to New York.
3. I need to hurry. I want to be home ________ time to watch the football game ________ television.
4. You have to get ________ the bus ________ the next stop if you want to go to the museum.
5. “Please pick me ________ at the station at 8 tomorrow morning.” “OK, but please be ________ time”
6. Look at those boys swimming ________ the river ________ the rain!
7. Did you see the notice ________ the bulletin board?

G それぞれの英文の状況に合うように、前の下線部分に前置詞 (on, at, by, in, along) を、後ろの下線には語群から語句を選んで文を完成させましょう。語句は一回しか使用できません。

✦ **語群** this road, chance, the door, my opinion, time, the traffic light, Shakespeare, fire

1. Look! That building is ________ __________________. We have to call the fire department.
2. Mary thought that movie was good, but ________ __________________ it wasn't good.
3. A cat ran out in front my car. I managed to stop just ________ __________________.
4. Have you ever read Romeo and Juliet ________ __________________?
5. We hadn't arranged to meet. We met ________ __________________.
6. Go ________ __________________, then turn left ________ __________________.
7. There is somebody knocking ________ __________________. Will you go and see who it is?

⋙ Listening Activity 09

H Dictation ⋙ Write what you hear.

1. In recent years, the number of ____________________________________ __________________.
2. Absolute poverty is a condition ________________________________ ________________________________.
3. Relative poverty is ____ ______.
4. It is unfortunate that, at the same time, ____________________ ____.

⋙ Another Challenge

I 大学生として、生活困窮家庭の子供を支援するためにどのような事ができるか考えてみましょう。

Unit 5 Empowering Women

女性のエンパワーメント

⋙ Warm-up Activities

A 下記の質問について話し合ってみましょう。

1. What do you think the women in the photograph above are doing?
2. Have you ever bought natural cosmetics containing ingredients made in developing countries?
3. Do you know of any environmental conservation activities?

B 下記の語句に該当する日本語を右から選び、その記号を（　）に書き入れましょう。

1. (　　) ingredient
2. (　　) transmit
3. (　　) extract
4. (　　) sustainable
5. (　　) conserve
6. (　　) sufficient
7. (　　) establish
8. (　　) ensure

(a) 抽出する
(b) 確実にする、保証する
(c) 保存する、保全する
(d) 設立する、制定する
(e) 原料、材料
(f) 送る、伝える、受け継ぐ
(g) 持続可能な
(h) 十分な

C Bに出てきた語句を（　）に入れて文を完成させてください。必要な場合は形を変えてください。

1. Just collecting money isn't (　　　　　　　　) to run a social enterprise.
2. Various projects are being (　　　　　　　　) for the conservation of the forests.

3. This restaurant serves a wide variety of vegetarian dishes using organic (   ).
4. With the help of computers, information can be (   ) to NPOs anywhere in the world.
5. The government is expected to (   ) that the people are safe and secure.

10

▩ Cosmetics, Forest Conservation, and Women's Empowerment

Over the past 10 to 20 years, the popularity of natural cosmetics containing natural ingredients, such as shea butter and argan oil, has become unwavering worldwide. Shea butter is extracted from the seeds of the shea tree (Vitellaria paradoxa), which is grown from West Africa to Central Africa, and argan oil is extracted from the seeds of the argan tree (Argania spinosa) that is grown in Morocco. Many other plant-based ingredients are used in natural cosmetics, and every year we find that more and more developing countries' names are listed as the origin of these ingredients. There are some projects to protect labor and the environment in those countries, and we can also support them by being aware of them in everyday life.

1. ____________________ 不動の、確固とした
2. ________________ 抽出する
3. ____________________ 発展途上国

Most of the plant-derived ingredients in cosmetics are extracted from seeds, flowers, and leaves, which is not a new technology. For example, oils and fats extracted from seeds have been widely used in daily life for a long time, such as for food and medicinal purposes. In developing countries, the collection and processing of seeds and leaves has traditionally been a woman's role, with the traditional extraction method passed down from mothers to their daughters over generations. In recent years, many international cooperation projects have been carried out to enable women to take the initiative in trading their products in the global market. This has been done through activities

4. ____________________ 植物由来
5. ________________ 薬用の
6. ________________ 加工
7. ________________ ～することを可能にさせる
8. ____________________ 主体となって行動する

such as organizing local women into production groups and training them in extraction methods that improve the quality of oils and fats.

In sustainable forest-management projects around the world, efforts are being made to stabilize local residents' livelihoods through the production of non-timber forest products (NTFP), which are gifts from the forest other than wood. The production of raw materials for cosmetics by the resident groups of women using seeds and leaves is one NTFP that is attracting attention. In order to conserve forests adequately, the livelihood of the residents must be stable enough to encourage them to protect forest resources. Their cooperation is also needed to prevent illegal logging and wildfires in large forests. By earning sufficient income from the forest, the residents are encouraged to actively protect the forest and use it sustainably.

By contributing to the local community and preserve the forests, many natural cosmetic manufacturers purchase products at a premium. This, however, has not always been true, and rules have been established to regulate companies in developed countries who make cosmetics from these raw materials. For example, companies need to comply with the Fair and Equitable Sharing of Benefits Arising from the Use of Genetic Resources[1] under the Nagoya Protocol[2]. The Nagoya Protocol ensures that profits from products made from plant-based raw materials that can be harvested only from their places of origin need to be distributed so that local workers can make a living and use the forest sustainably. Since natural cosmetics often use ingredients from fair trade and community trade[3], they clearly reflect the relationship between the producer and the natural environment.

9. ______________ 組織化する

10. ______________ 安定させる

11. ______________ 生計

12. ______________ 非木材

13. ______________ 適切に

14. ______________ 資源

15. ______________ 不法の

16. ______________ 伐採、材木切り出し

17. ______________ 貢献する

18. ______________ 保存する、保全する

19. ______________ 製造業者、メーカー

20. ______________ 高い値段で

21. ______________ ～に従う

22. ______________ 利益

23. ______________ 収穫する

24. ______________ 反映する

In short, people should put more thought into what they buy. By choosing products from companies that actively promote fair-trade practices, we can support forest conservation and improve women's income in developing countries.

(533 words)

✦ **Notes / 注**

1. Fair and Equitable Sharing of Benefits Arising from the Use of Genetic Resources: 遺伝子資源の利用から生ずる利益の公正かつ均等な配分
2. Nagoya Protocol: 名古屋議定書
3. community trade: コミュニティートレード（特定の地域・コミュニティと持続的に公正な取引（フェアトレード）を継続することでその地域の人々を支えるシステム）

≫ Comprehension Check

D 内容に関する文を完成させるために、最も適切なものを選んでください。

1. Which is true about natural cosmetics?

A. Ingredients for natural cosmetics are grown only in developed countries.

B. Without using ingredients from fair trade and community trade, natural cosmetics might not clearly represent the relationship between the producer and the natural environment.

C. Traditionally, fathers have passed down knowledge and skills to extract oil and fats from plants to sons in many developing countries.

D. Argan oil is extracted from shea trees that are mainly grown in Morocco.

2. Which of the following has NOT been done to enable women to take the initiative in trading their products globally?

A. Many international cooperation projects over the past few years

B. Activities to organize local women into production groups

C. Sustainable forest-management projects around the world

D. Training for women in extraction methods that improve the quality of oils and fats

3. Why is it important to stabilize the livelihoods of the local residents?

A. Because the residents must take expensive measures against wildfires.

B. Because they want to buy a lot of seeds and leaves to produce natural cosmetics.

C. Because they need money to buy equipment for illegal logging.

D. Because their stable livelihoods encourage the residents to actively protect the forest and use it sustainably.

4. What should natural cosmetic manufacturers do to contribute to the local community and preserve the forests?

A. They should ensure the fair distribution of profits from products made from raw materials.

B. They should purchase raw materials at low prices to offer reasonable products.

C. They should maintain traditional ways to extract ingredients from plants.

D. They should establish rules so that they can gain as much profit as possible.

5. Which of the following does NOT support forest conservation and improve women's income in developing countries?

A. Buying natural cosmetics using ingredients from community trade

B. Choosing products from companies that actively promote fair-trade practices

C. Being aware of labor and the environment in developing countries

D. Ignoring the relationship between the producer and the natural environment

≫ Summary

E (　　) にあてはまる語句を語群から選んで入れて、本文の要約を完成させてください。

Natural cosmetics have been becoming popular worldwide. Some projects (1.　　) labor and the environment in developing countries that are the origins of plant-based (2.　　) for natural cosmetics. In developing countries, women are engaged in (3.　　) these (2.　　) from plants. Many international cooperation projects have been (4.　　) to enable women to take the initiative in trading their products in the global market. In addition, efforts to (5.　　) the residents' livelihoods are being made to conserve the forests. (6.　　) income from the forest's blessings allows the residents to protect the forest and use it (7.　　). Furthermore, rules have been (8.　　) to protect people who make cosmetics from raw materials. Many natural cosmetic manufacturers purchase products at a premium to (9.　　) to the local community and (10.　　) the forests. By choosing products from companies that actively promote fair-trade practices, we can support forest conservation and improve women's income in developing countries.

✦ **語群**

a. contribute	b. sufficient	c. protect	d. preserve	e. ingredients
f. carried out	g. extracting	h. sustainably	i. stabilize	j. established

≫ Writing Activities < 助動詞 auxiliary>

F 日本語の意味になるように、(　　) 内の語句を並び替えましょう。

1. 企業は発展途上国の労働者に適切な労働条件を確保することを約束するべきです。

   (for workers / commit / should / ensuring / to / appropriate / companies / working conditions) in developing countries.

   ____

2. フェアトレードは私たちの社会や環境に良い影響を与えることができます。

   (have / on / and / can / positive / our society / fair trade / impacts / environment).

   ____

3. 女性の収入を向上させるために、女性たちは国際市場で彼女たちの製品を主体となって取引きしなければなりません。
(their products / the global market / the initiative / in / take / must / trading / in / women) to improve their income.

____

G 次の日本語の文を英語にしましょう。

1. 田中さんはまだここに到着していません。彼は電車に乗り遅れたに違いありません。

____

2. 私と一緒に写真を撮ってもらえませんか。

____

≫ Listening Activity 11

H Dictation ≫ Write what you hear.

1. In order to support developing countries, ____________________
____________________________ in our daily life.

2. Many international cooperation projects ____________________
____________________ in trading their products worldwide.

3. It is important to stabilize the livelihood of the residents so that ___
____________________________.

4. If you would like to support forest conservation and improve women's income in developing countries, ____________________________
______________________________________.

⋙ Another Challenge

I Fair trade や Community trade について調べてみましょう。

✍

Unit 6 Sport Psychology

スポーツ心理学

⋙ Warm-up Activities

A 下記の質問について話し合ってみましょう。

1. Have you ever heard of sport psychology before?
2. What do you think athletes need to do to win?
3. What can you do to improve your mental strength?

B 下記の語句に該当する日本語を右から選び、その記号を（　）に書き入れましょう。

1. (　　) achieve
2. (　　) competition
3. (　　) enhancement
4. (　　) anxiety
5. (　　) respiration
6. (　　) stable
7. (　　) issue
8. (　　) appropriate

(a) 不安
(b) 適切な
(c) 達成する
(d) 問題
(e) 競技
(f) 向上
(g) 呼吸
(h) 安定した

C Bに出てきた語句を（　）に入れて文を完成させてください。必要な場合は形を変えてください。

1. The (　　　　　　　　　　) of the region is inseparable from the security of our country.
2. She (　　　　　　　　　　) good results in the sales department.

3. Winners of these (   ) will go to the finals which will be held in Hyogo.
4. We agree that the voice of low-income nations should be (   ).
5. This textbook is (   ) for an intermediate-level student.

Sport Psychology for Athletes 12

There are many top athletes in Japan, both Olympic and those in professional sports, who give us hope and inspiration as they compete at the pinnacle in their fields. It goes without saying that all top-class athletes competing at the peak of their chosen sports have achieved a top level of physical strength and technique. While claims that “the crowd cheering helped me give 120%” are certainly feasible, fundamentally, the deciding factor between victory and defeat is just how well, based on their many hours of training and preparation, these athletes can display the very best of their true abilities under the pressure of actual competition. That is where mental strength can become an important weapon.

In recent years, in addition to technical and physical training, sport psychology has become more recognized worldwide as an essential aspect of performance enhancement among elite athletes. Mental training is onc of the most well-known representative approaches in the field of sport psychology. Various approaches are used for mental training skills, such as relaxation, goal-setting, visualization and self-talk. For mental training to be effective, it is important to assess individual athletes’ needs as a first step and choose the appropriate skills to overcome any challenges.

1. ________________ 運動選手
2. ________________ 頂点
3. ________________ 強さ
4. ________________ 敗北
5. ________________ 発揮する
6. ________________ 認識する
7. ________________ 代表的な
8. ________________ 効果的な

For example, breathing techniques help to relax and avoid excessive performance anxiety under high pressure. To do this, athletes use a biofeedback device (Kinect) to visualize physical reactions such as the transition of parasympathetic nerves and respiration rates during relaxation training (Fig. 1, Fig. 2). In this way, athletes can see the effects of training as a process, which helps them acquire precise breathing (Fig. 3, Fig. 4).

9. ________________ 過剰な

10. ________________ 視覚化する

11. ________________ 身につける、獲得する

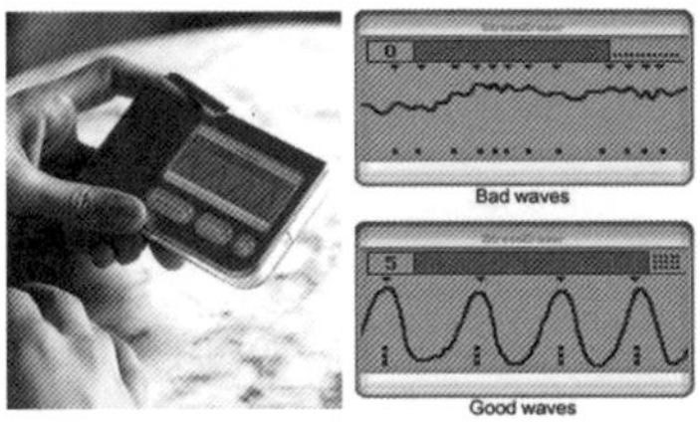

Fig1. Stress Eraser and the examples of bad waves and good waves.

Figure 2: Kinect

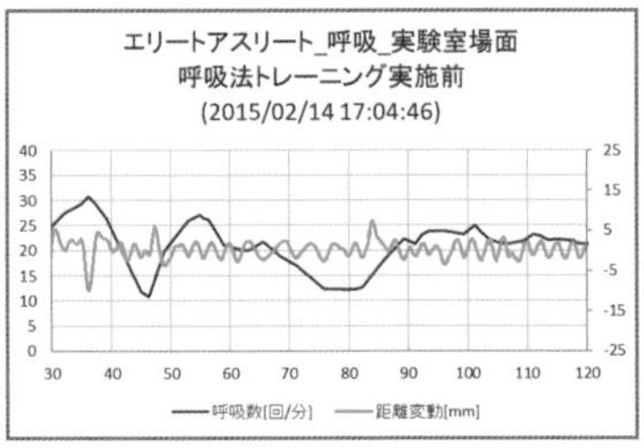

Fig3: Respiration Rate During Breathing Exercise in Lab 1.

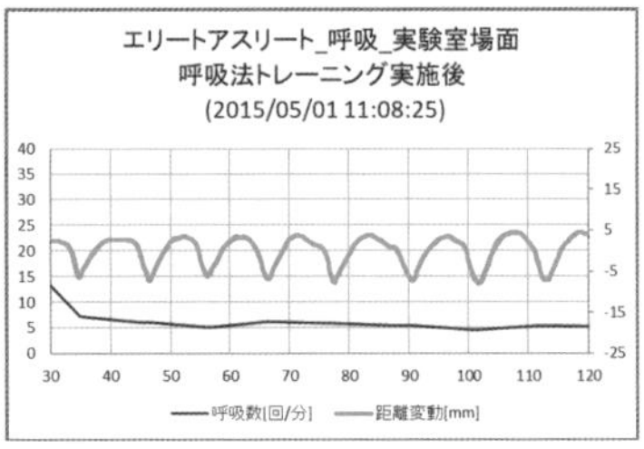

Fig4: Respiration Rate During Breathing Exercise in Lab 2.

Looking at Figures 3 and 4 above, the blue line quantifies the movement of the chest during breathing, while the black line represents the number of breaths. The horizontal axis in the figures shows the passage of time, the right vertical axis shows the distance of chest movement [mm], and the left vertical axis shows the number of breaths per minute. Figure 3 represents the subject's data before training, and it seems that they cannot control their breathing. After taking proper breathing exercises, as shown in Figure 4, the subject could properly

12. ________________ 数値化する

13. ________________ 水平の（横の）

14. ________________ 垂直の（縦の）

15. ________________ 適切な

control their breathing: the distance change is stable between -5 and +5 and the number of breaths is well controlled around 5 times per minute. Athletes continue training with breathing techniques until they can reach their optimal concentration and relaxation prior to their performance in actual sport situations.

16. ______________ 最適な

17. ______________ ～より前に

Thus, sports psychology is the study of how psychology influences sports, athletic performance, and exercise. One of the goals is to clarify the issues related to sport from a psychological aspect so as to solve the issues and improve performance. In addition, sport psychology also plays an important role in gaining a deeper understanding of humans from both psychological and physical aspects, focusing on the intimate connection between the mind and body. Understanding one's own pain, accepting anxiety and pressure, supporting oneself, moving forward, etc. are the foundations of supporting and living with others. (503 words)

18. ______________ 明らかにする

19. ______________ 緊密な

20. ______________ 基盤

≫ Comprehension Check

D 内容に関する文を完成させるために、最も適切なものを選んでください。

1. Which is true regarding top athletes?

A. We receive hope and inspiration as we see top athletes compete for victory under pressure.

B. It is likely that top athletes cannot achieve a top level of physical strength without a cheering crowd.

C. The size of the cheering crowd is the sole deciding factor between victory and defeat.

D. Top athletes are those who do not feel pressure under any circumstance.

2. Which is true regarding mental training?

A. With mental training, athletes need to carry out less technical and physical training activities.

B. The importance of mental training has become more widely recognized recently.

C. Mental training is very effective for every athlete so that individual needs are not important.

D. Goal-setting is the most important approach among many mental training techniques.

3. Which is true regarding the process or effectiveness of mental training?

A. Excessive anxiety caused by mental training enhances an athlete's performance.

B. Athletes can reduce performance anxiety by acquiring the ability to control their breathing.

C. It is still difficult to visualize what happens inside an athlete's body as a result of mental training.

D. The effectiveness of mental training cannot be confirmed until we see the athlete's results.

4. Which is true regarding breath control training?

A. Both passage of time and chest movement are represented vertically in the figures.

B. Figure 3 shows that the movement of the chest and the number of breaths are not correlated.

C. Few athletes become able to control their breathing even after taking breath control training.

D. It is more effective to take breath control training right after an actual sport event.

5. Which is true regarding sport psychology?

A. Sport psychology studies how sports influence an athlete's mind in actual sport situations.

B. Sport psychology tries to understand the relation between the mind and body for both athletes and nonathletes.

C. Sport psychology is exclusively interested in sports, so it has little connection to nonathletes.

D. The harmony among people has greatly contributed to the development of sport psychology.

⋙ Summary

E (　　) にあてはまる語句を語群から選んで入れて、本文の要約を完成させてください。

In order for athletes to show the very best of their true abilities under the pressure of (1.　　) competition, they need to be strong mentally as well as physically. Mental training, the best known (2.　　) sport psychology has offered, is widely utilized to (3.　　) such a purpose. By finding out each athlete's needs and choosing the most (4.　　) method, it helps them overcome the challenges they face. Nowadays athletes use biofeedback (5.　　) that visualize the effect of their training. They (6.　　), for example, breathing control training before actual competition (7.　　) they reach their best concentration and relaxation (8.　　). More importantly, sport psychology is of (9.　　) not only for athletes but also for all of us in that both physical and psychological health is the foundation of a better life.

✦ **語群**

a. continue	b. appropriate	c. fulfill	d. until	e. state
f. approach	g. devices	h. significance	i. actual	

⋙ Writing Activities < 疑問詞 interrogative>

F 日本語の意味になるように、(　　) 内の語句を並び替えましょう。

1. 問題はこの庭のどこに種を植えるかということだ。

   (is / question / sow / the / the seeds / to / where) in this garden.

2. フェアトレードは私たちの社会や環境に良い誰のアドバイスなら信用するかと問われたが、誰もその質問に答えなかった。影響を与えることができます。

   (advice / asked / they / trust / when / whose / would) , none of them responded to the question.

3. お母さんの病気はいつからか？

   (been / has / ill / mother / since / when / your) in bed?

G 日本語の意味になるように、(　　) 内に入る適切な語句を選びましょう。

1. この試験に合格しなければどうなるのか？

   (　　　) we should fail to pass this examination?

   a. How does it happen　b. How about　c. What happens　d. What if

2. 次の土曜日にテニスをするのはどう？

   (　　　　　　　　　　) playing tennis next Saturday?

   a. How come about　b. How are you　c. What do you say to
   d. What would you tell about

≫ Listening Activity 13

H Dictation ≫ Write what you hear.

1. The difference in mental strength could be ________________________ ________________ in top level competition.

2. ____ such as relaxation, goal-setting, image training and self-talk.

3. The difference in ______________________________ before and after taking training is seen in Figures 3 and 4, respectively.

4. One of the goals that sport psychology has been pursuing is _______ _______________________ between the mind and body.

≫ Another Challenge

I メンタルトレーニングには本文で紹介されている呼吸法のトレーニング以外にどのようなトレーニングがあるか調べてみましょう。

Unit 7

I Don't Have Money but Need Treatment

十分なお金はないけれど、治療を受けたい

≫ Warm-up Activities

A 下記の質問について話し合ってみましょう。

1. Have you ever called 119 in an emergency?
2. Who needs to pay the full cost of medical expenses in Japan?
3. Where is the closest free/low-cost clinic to where you live?

B 下記の語句に該当する日本語を右から選び、その記号を（　）に書き入れましょう。

1. (　　) insurance
2. (　　) expense
3. (　　) clinic
4. (　　) ambulance
5. (　　) low-cost
6. (　　) emergency
7. (　　) municipality
8. (　　) prescription

(a) 診療所
(b) 安価の
(c) 費用、出費
(d) 自治体、市当局
(e) 保険
(f) 処方箋、処方された薬
(g) 救急車
(h) 緊急事態

C Bに出てきた語句を（　）に入れて文を完成させてください。必要な場合は形を変えてください。

1. Dial 119 and ask for an (　　　　　　　　).
2. (　　　　　　　　) provide services such as electricity, water and rubbish collection.

3. This medicine is freely available without a (   ).
4. This door should only be used in an (   ).
5. You shouldn't forget to take the cost of (   ) into consideration.

I Don't Have Enough Money, but I Need Treatment

Suppose you had a severe headache or stomachache in the middle of the night. You could wake someone up in your family and have them drive you to the hospital. Or, in case of an emergency, you could dial 119 to call an ambulance, which might be easier for you and the natural thing to do. However, one of the reasons why you would think like this is because Japan has a national health insurance system[1], so you do not have to worry too much about the cost of treatment. Now, imagine a situation like this: you want to have medical treatment, but you don't have enough money. What would you do in this situation?

1. ________________ ～へ電話をかける

We take it for granted in Japan that anyone can pay less than the actual cost of medical expenses by showing their health insurance ID card at the hospital counter. All people living in Japan except foreigners on a short stay and most public-assistance recipients are insured by some kind of national health insurance that reduces out-of-pocket costs for medical treatment. However, there are situations where, even in Japan, people need to pay the full cost of medical expenses.

2. ________________ 受給者
3. ________________ ～に保険を掛ける
4. ________________ 自己負担費

For example, if you fail to pay your insurance premium for too long, the hospital will decline your insurance and you may have to pay the full amount of the expenses unless you pay the overdue amount. How can you pay the full amount of medical expenses when you cannot even pay for insurance?

5. ________________ 保険料
6. ________________ 期限が過ぎて

Another example is people without access to health insurance, such as those who are escaping domestic violence and need to stay at internet cafes with very little cash, or the homeless, who often do not have a health insurance card to show to a medical institution. These people are very unlikely to receive subsidized medical expenses. Indeed, for some of these people, even if they were able to show a health insurance ID card, some would not be able to afford even the decreased co-payments. So, while Japan has a national health insurance system, there are still some people who fall through the cracks.

7. ______________ 家庭内暴力

8. ______________ (金銭的) 余裕がある

9. ______________ 自己負担分

10. ______________ すき間

Fortunately, if you need medical treatment but do not have any money to pay for it, depending on your financial situation, there are clinics that offer free or low-cost consultations. There are 703 free/low-cost clinics and they were used by about 7.61 million people in Japan in 2018. In each clinic, a medical social worker is provided so that patients can receive not only medical treatment, but also consultations about their lives. Medical social workers can connect the patients with the social resources that they need.

11. ______________ 診察

However, not all the problems the patients have will necessarily be solved by free or low-cost clinics. For example, in the case where you need to be on medication, it is unlikely that medicine will be free or low-cost if the clinic does not offer prescriptions from their in-house pharmacy. This is because health insurance pharmacies do not cover charges for medicine under this system. Only a handful of municipalities, such as Asahikawa, Aomori, Kochi, and Naha, assist in the cost for medicine. Furthermore, municipalities do not have to establish a free/low-cost clinic. This means that

12. ______________ 必ず

13. ______________ 治療

14. ______________ 薬局

15. ______________ 一握りの

16. ______________ 設置する

the municipality you live in will not necessarily have one available. Nevertheless, knowing the closest free/low-cost clinic to where you live is just as important as knowing how to call an ambulance. That knowledge may save you and your loved ones. (574 words)

17. ______________ 利用できる、手に入る

✦ Notes / 注

1. national health insurance system: 国民皆保険制度

⋙ Comprehension Check

D 内容に関する文を完成させるために、最も適切なものを選んでください。

1. What do Japanese people take for granted?

A. Everyone has to pay the full cost of medical expenses.

B. Everyone in Japan is insured by some kind of national health insurance that increases out-of-pocket costs for medical treatment.

C. Anyone can pay less than the actual cost of medical expenses by showing their health insurance ID card at the hospital counter.

D. Anyone can avoid paying any medical expenses by showing their health insurance ID card at the hospital counter.

2. Who needs to pay the full cost of medical expenses in Japan?

A. People who cannot pay for insurance

B. People who are in the hospital

C. People who pay the overdue insurance payment

D. People who are able to show a health insurance ID card

3. What is the meaning of "there are still some people who fall through the cracks" in the third paragraph?

A. Some people cannot pay for insurance.

B. Some people cannot show a health insurance ID card.

C. Some people do not have any money.

D. Some people cannot have the benefit of a national health insurance system.

4. According to the article, what are free/low-cost clinics?

A. In free/low-cost clinics, you are required to bring some money.

B. In free/low-cost clinics, you can only receive medical treatment.

C. In free/low-cost clinics, you can get medical treatment even if you do not have any money.

D. In free/low-cost clinics, you have to pay the full cost of medical expenses.

5. Which of the following is suggested in the last paragraph?

A. There are some problems which cannot be solved by free/low-cost clinics.

B. All problems can be solved by free/low-cost clinics.

C. Medicine should be free in free/low-cost clinics.

D. All of the free/low-cost clinics should offer prescriptions from their in-house pharmacy.

⋙ Summary

E (　) にあてはまる語句を語群から選んで入れて、本文の要約を完成させてください。

We take it for (1.　　) in Japan that anyone can pay less than the actual cost of medical (2.　　) by showing their health (3.　　) ID card at the hospital counter. However, there are situations where, even in Japan, people need to pay the full cost of medical expenses. If you need medical (4.　　) but do not have any money to pay for it, depending on your (5.　　) situation, there are clinics that offer free or low-cost (6.　　). However, not all the problems that patients have will (7.　　) be solved by free or low-cost clinics. Nevertheless, knowing the (8.　　) free/low-cost clinic to where you live is just as (9.　　) as knowing how to call an (10.　　). That knowledge may save you and your loved ones.

✦ **語群**

a. treatment	b. necessarily	c. expenses	d. important	e. financial
f. ambulance	g. granted	h. consultations	i. insurance	j. closest

⋙ Writing Activities < 接続詞 conjuncts>

F 日本語の意味になるように、(　　) 内の語句を並び替えましょう。
ただし、接続詞が不足しているので本文で使われている接続詞を 1 語補いなさい。

1. もし明日雨が降れば、私は家にいます。
   (home / stay / it / will / rains / I / tomorrow,).

   ____

2. 成功していたかもしれないのに、あなたはどうしてあきらめてしまったのか。
   Why (succeeded / give up / might have / did / trying, / you / you)?

   ____

3. 1人で旅をするのが好きな人もいる一方、友人と旅をするのが好きな人もいる。
   Some people (with their friends / like to / others / alone, / traveling / travel / prefer).

   ____

G 日本語の意味になるように、(　　) 内に適切な語句を入れましょう。

1. 食べ物は人生の長さだけでなく、人生の質にも影響を与えます。
   The food you eat influences not (　　　) the length of your life (　　　) (　　　) the quality of your life.
2. 彼女は前払いをしなければ、何もしません。
   She won't do anything (　　　) you pay her in advance.
3. 試合は雨でも予定通り決行します。
   The game will be held as scheduled (　　　) (　　　) it rains.

≫ Listening Activity 15

H Dictation ≫ Write what you hear.

1. Except for foreigners on a short visit and most recipients of public assistance, ____

   ____________________________.

2. In some cases, ____

   ________, they couldn't afford the decreased co-payments.

3. A medical social worker is available in each clinic __________

   ____

   ____________.

4. When you need to be on medication, ____________________________

   ____.

≫ Another Challenge

I 自分の身近な無料・低額診療所について調べてみましょう。どこでどのような診断を行っているのか、まとめてみましょう。

Unit 8 LGBTQ+

LGBTQ+

≫ Warm-up Activities

A 下記の質問について話し合ってみましょう。

1. Do you know what the flag in the picture represents?
2. What sort of establishment is shown in the picture?
3. Why would this flag be flown here?

B 下記の語句に該当する日本語を右から選び、その記号を（　）に書き入れましょう。

1. (　　) diverse
2. (　　) heterosexual
3. (　　) indicate
4. (　　) due to
5. (　　) minority
6. (　　) sexual orientation
7. (　　) gender-identity
8. (　　) awareness

(a) ～のため、～の結果
(b) 少数、少数派
(c) 表す、意図する
(d) 意識、気付き
(e) 性自認
(f) 異性愛の
(g) 多様な
(h) 性的指向

C Bに出てきた語句を（　　）に入れて文を完成させてください。必要な場合は形を変えてください。

1. The activities that our professor is engaging in are very (　　　　　　　　).
2. The school excursion was postponed (　　　　　　　　　) rain.

3. ( ) is the self-aware concept of "how you perceive your own sex."

4. A ( ) refers to people who are, particularly socially, regarded as a small group.

5. Statistics ( ) that our living standard has not improved for 30 years.

LGBTQ+ and KG Rainbow Week 16

LGBTQ+ stands for lesbian, gay, bisexual, transgender, queer[1] (or sometimes questioning[2]), and "plus," which represents a diverse range of sexual orientations and gender-identities, referring to anyone who is non-cisgender[3] or non-heterosexual. According to the results of an online survey conducted in 2019, about 10% of 348,000 valid respondents identified themselves as LGBTQ+. Another survey conducted in the same period on 2,578 people, however, indicated that 83.9% said that they were not aware of any LGBTQ+ people around them. This is because about 78% of LGBTQ+ people or sexual minorities have not been able to tell anyone about their sexual orientation or gender identity due to the social environment that they are in.

The reason why LGBTQ+ people have not been able to reveal their sexuality in Japan is that the human rights of LGBTQ+ people have not yet been fully protected in Japanese society. On the one hand, according to another online survey, about a quarter of LGBTQ+ people in Japan have experienced "outing"—having their sexuality disclosed to others without their consent. On the other hand, of the 8,690 respondents, 78.9% said that they have heard discriminatory speech about sexual minorities at work or school. About half of LGBTQ+ people responded by saying that governments, companies, and schools should

1. ____________ 表す
2. ____________ 指向
3. ____________ 有効な
4. ____________ 回答者
5. ____________ ～に気付いて
6. ____________ 性自認
7. ____________ 明らかにする
8. ____________ 同意
9. ____________ 差別的な

make greater efforts to make a better environment for their community. Only 12% said that their companies or schools had educational programs for employees to improve the understanding of LGBTQ+, which points to the limited protection they receive in Japanese society.

Kwansei Gakuin University (KGU) is one of the Japanese universities that recognized this issue early on and have been making efforts to make a better environment for their students and employees. KGU has been offering undergraduate courses such as Sexuality and Human Rights since 2003 and has held an annual human rights lecture on sexual diversity since 2006. Although these courses and lectures provide opportunities for students and employees to learn about the experiences of LGBTQ+ people, it seems to be difficult for most of them to realize that it is an issue on campus and that they themselves may hurt LGBTQ+ classmates by casually asking their classmates if they have a boyfriend or girlfriend.

In response to this situation, the KGU Institute of Human Rights Research and Education started to hold an annual event called KG Rainbow Week in 2013 to improve its campus atmosphere and university policies to respect sexual diversity. This event has various activities, such as movie showings, LGBTQ+ book exhibits, panel exhibits, and panel discussions organized by LGBTQ+ students to raise awareness about sexual diversity. In addition, it also advocates the needs of LGBTQ+ students to university officials by conducting online surveys on issues experienced by LGBTQ+ students on campus and then making suggestions about how to make the KGU community better. If the KG Rainbow

10. ________________ 努力

11. ________________ 改善する

12. ________________ 早い時期に

13. ________________ 年一回の

14. ________________ 機会

15. ________________ 何気なく

16. ________________ 雰囲気

17. ________________ 方針、方策

18. ________________ 高める

19. ________________ 唱える

20. ________________ 課題、問題

Week event can make each person studying and working at KGU recognize and respect sexual diversity on campus, the university will become an even better environment for everyone who studies and works there.

(505 words)

✦ **Notes/ 注**

1. Queer: クィア（異性愛者・シスジェンダーではない人たちの総称）
2. Questioning: クエスチョニング（自分の性的指向、性自認、あるいは性表現に対して疑問をもったり、考えている過程にある人）
3. Cisgender: シスジェンダー（生まれた際に割り当てられた性別と、性自認が一致している人）

⋙ Comprehension Check

D 内容に関する文を完成させるために、最も適切なものを選んでください。

1. Why is the author writing this article?

A. To increase awareness of LGBTQ+ people around the world

B. To show what KGU is doing to support LGBTQ+ people on campus

C. To get more LGBTQ+ people to come to KGU

D. To get more paying customers to come to join Rainbow Week

2. What do the three surveys tell us?

A. 348,000 people identified as LGBTQ+, 60% of people said they weren't aware of LGBTQ+, and a quarter of LGBTQ+ people haven't experienced 'outing.'

B. About 25% of people have experienced 'outing,' about 80% say they weren't aware of LGBTQ+ people around them, and 34,800 people identify as LGBTQ+.

C. 83.9% of people said they weren't aware of LGBTQ+ people around them, 348,000 people identified as LGBTQ+, and a quarter of LGBTQ+ people haven't experienced 'outing.'

D. About 25% of people have experienced "outing," about eight percent say they weren't aware of LGBTQ+ people around them, and 348,000 people identify as LGBTQ+.

3. KGU has made efforts to make a better environment for LGBTQ+ people, but what issue still exists on campus?

A. There aren't enough surveys being conducted on campus.

B. Rainbow Week needs more members.

C. KGU doesn't have enough money to support Rainbow Week activities.

D. Many people don't know that they have hurt their LGBTQ+ classmates in some way.

4. Other than movie showings, book exhibits, panel exhibits and panel discussions, what else does KG Rainbow Week do for LGBTQ+ students?

A. They conduct online surveys about issues experienced by LGBTQ+ students.

B. They invite famous LGBTQ+ people to talk at the event.

C. They ask non-LGBTQ+ students to join.

D. They raise money for the next year's event by asking for donations.

5. What is the purpose of the surveys?

A. To find out how people respect sexual diversity

B. To recognize the hard work during rainbow week

C. To make the environment better on campus for LGBTQ+ people

D. To find out what each person is studying

≫ Summary

E (　　) にあてはまる語句を語群から選んで入れて、本文の要約を完成させてください。

Ten percent of people from an online survey said that they identify as (1.　　), which stands for lesbian, gay, bisexual, transgender, queer and plus. However, another survey showed that people are not aware of LGBTQ+ people around them. This is because it is difficult for LGBTQ+ people to (2.　　) their sexual identity in today's (3.　　). In order to make LGBTQ+ people feel more (4.　　) and open to (5.　　) their sexuality, Kwansei Gakuin University has an (6.　　) called "KG Rainbow Week." During this week there are many different activities for people to learn more about LGBTQ+ and raise (7.　　) about what problems the LGBTQ+ community may face. Through this event, they are trying to (8.　　) campus life for everyone who studies and (9.　　) there.

✦ **語群**

a. express	b. event	c. awareness	d. LGBTQ+	e. works
f. reveal	g. comfortable	h. environment	i. improve	

≫ Writing Activities < 関係詞 relatives>

F 日本語の意味になるように、(　　) 内の語句を並び替えましょう。

1. 彼女の叔父は京都に住んでいるが、先日彼女を訪ねてきた。
   Her uncle, (her / to / in / who / Kyoto, / lives / visit / came) the other day.

   ____

2. この記事を書いた人は学生です。
   The person (student / is / this / who / a / wrote / article).

   ____

3. サムがくれた本は面白かった。
   (which / to / me / Sam / the / gave / book) was interesting.

   ____

G 次の２つの英文を、関係代名詞を使って１つの文にしてみましょう。

1. Mr. Haugh comes from New Zealand. He wrote this essay.

____

2. Mary received a long letter from John. She read the letter repeatedly.

____

≫ Listening Activity 17

H -1 Listen and fill in the blanks in each question. Then choose the best answer.

1. What (　　　　　　) (　　　　) activities are run (　　　　　　) KG Rainbow Week?

A. There are three reasons.

B. There is a huge buffet, panel discussions, and games.

C. There are various activities, such as movie showings, LGBTQ+ book exhibits, etc.

D. There are various events that aren't run at KG Rainbow Week.

2. Why are so (　　　　　　　　) not aware of LGBTQ+ (　　　　　　　　) around them?

A. Because there aren't that many of them.

B. Because LGBTQ+ people don't feel comfortable revealing their sexuality.

C. Because KGU is not doing enough.

D. Because KG Rainbow Week only happens once a week.

3. How is KGU trying to (　　　　　) the situation for LGBTQ+ (　　　　　)?

A. They are asking the government to conduct more surveys.

B. They are trying to find as many LGBTQ+ people as possible.

C. They are trying to get the laws changed for LGBTQ+ people.

D. They are holding KG Rainbow Week once a year.

H -2 Dictation ≫ Write what you hear.

1. ______________________________ of any LGBTQ+ people around them.

2. To improve this situation, the KGU Institute of Human Rights Research and Education ______________________________
______________.

3. About half of LGBTQ+ people responded by saying that governments, companies, and schools ______________________________
______________________.

4. This event has various activities, such as movie showings, LGBTQ+ book exhibits, ______________________________
____________.

≫ Another Challenge

I 海外におけるLGBTQ+への制度や対応について調べてみましょう。

Unit 9 Healthy Bones

骨の健康のために

≫ Warm-up Activities

A 下記の質問について話し合ってみましょう。

1. What can we learn from the space program?
2. What happens to our bodies when humans spend a long time in space?
3. What do we need to do to keep our bones healthy?

B 下記の語句に該当する日本語を右から選び、その記号を（　）に書き入れましょう。

1. (　　) opportunity
2. (　　) sufficient
3. (　　) maintain
4. (　　) strengthen
5. (　　) weightless
6. (　　) occur
7. (　　) require
8. (　　) engage in

(a) ～に取り組む
(b) 生じる、起こる
(c) 必要とする
(d) 無重力の
(e) 維持する
(f) 機会
(g) 強化する
(h) 十分な

C Bに出てきた語句を（　　）に入れて文を完成させてください。必要な場合は形を変えてください。

1. There wasn't (　　　　　　　　) evidence to show that the new proposal would be better.
2. A dialogue forum has been set up to (　　　　　　　　) relations between the two countries.

3. There are not so many ( ) for students to speak English outside the classroom.
4. Yesterday a good idea ( ) to me when I was walking along the river.
5. Employees were ( ) to submit a brief summary of the meeting.

▩ For Our Bone Health—Messages from Outer Space 18

In 1977, NASA launched two spacecraft, Voyager 1 and Voyager 2, into space. They visited Jupiter, Saturn, Uranus and Neptune, and sent large amounts of data back to Earth. In fact, the Voyagers and other unmanned spacecraft have continued to travel even beyond our solar system. On the other hand, although NASA's Apollo Program successfully landed the first man on the moon in 1969, we have yet to travel beyond that point, and crewed missions have so far been restricted to only traveling to the moon. What makes it difficult for mankind to travel further than the moon?

1. ______________ 打ち上げる
2. ______________ 無人の
3. ______________ 着陸させる
4. ______________ 有人の
5. ______________ 限られている

The reason is that the human body is not able to maintain normal physiological activity when living in a weightless environment for an extended period of time. One well-known phenomenon is muscle atrophy[1] that occurs due to extended stays in weightless space. Another, perhaps more dangerous, side effect of weightlessness is the loss of calcium from bone tissue. Although calcium loss in bone tissue due to weightlessness is still under research, one thing that is clear is that mechanical stress[2] on bone, such as lifting, bending and twisting, and even just supporting one's own weight when standing is important for strengthening bone tissue. The mechanical stress we experience due to gravity on Earth is sufficient to maintain healthy bones. However, in the weightlessness of space,

6. ______________ 生理的な
7. ______________ 現象
8. ______________ （細胞）組織
9. ______________ 曲げる
10. ______________ 重力

our healthy bones cannot be sustained as it is difficult to continuously perform exercises that subject them to such mechanical stress. This inability to maintain healthy bones is one of the main reasons why mankind has only reached the moon, while other unmanned spacecrafts have been flying out of the solar system.

In space, moderate mechanical stress, especially from sports, is just as important for maintaining healthy bones as on Earth. Mechanical stress can be represented as an impact load[3]—which is our body's ability to resist a force applied externally in a very short period of time. Athletes who play sports with large impact loads have increased bone density. These kinds of sports are those that experience collision and contact, such as judo, rugby and football. We all know that collision and contact sports are often painful, but the impact load that causes this pain applies mechanical stress to the bone tissue and strengthens it.

Moderate exercise on Earth can also help prevent osteoporosis[4], a disease in which the flux of calcium from bone tissue reduces bone strength and increases the chances of bone fractures. The changes are similar in bones in zero gravity space and those in osteoporosis patients on Earth. Osteoporosis progresses with aging and occurs frequently in the elderly. The most important thing to do to prevent osteoporosis is moderate exercise with a strong impact load at a young age. This process gives us adequate bone density, and it is necessary to continue physical activity over the course of one's life to maintain it.

As you can see, space offers mankind many opportunities to learn about itself, the planet we are living on, and ways to maintain our healthy

11. ________________ 維持する

12. ________________ 不能

13. ________________ 適度な

14. ________________ 耐える、抵抗する

15. ________________ 衝突

16. ________________ 流出

17. ________________ 進行する

18. ________________ 頻繁に

bones. Whether in space or on Earth, exercise is an important part of maintaining good health. Let's improve our mental and physical health by engaging in proper exercises that will lead to a happier life! (541 words)

19. ______________ 運動

✦ Notes / 注

1. Muscle atrophy: 筋萎縮（加齢、 栄養失調、 その他さまざまな怪我や病気により生じる筋肉量の低下）
2. Mechanical stress: 機械的応力（外部から力が加えられる際にそれに対して体内や物体の内部で生じる力）
3. Impact load: 衝撃荷重（物体が別の物体に衝撃を与える時に急激かつ短時間に作用する負荷）
4. Osteoporosis: 骨粗鬆症（骨密度の低下により骨が弱くなり骨折しやすくなる病気）

⋙ Comprehension Check

D 内容に関する文を完成させるために、最も適切なものを選んでください。

1. What does the first paragraph tell us?

A. The Voyagers are coming back to the Earth after traveling around Saturn, Uranus and Neptune.

B. NASA launched the Voyagers to investigate the moon before the first man landed there.

C. The Voyagers were the second manned spacecraft after the Apollo Program in 1969.

D. The moon has been the furthest place in space human beings have ever landed so far.

2. Which is true regarding the potential problems for man in space?

A. In a weightless environment, muscle atrophy causes bone tissue to lose calcium.

B. Calcium loss in bones leads to the weakening or loss of muscle, which is called muscle atrophy.

C. Muscle atrophy may be the second most dangerous phenomenon in a weightless environment.

D. The problem of calcium loss in bone has been solved so that it is no longer an issue.

3. Which sentence explains the nature of mechanical stress best?

A. The mechanical stress that man experiences in space is harmful to our bodies, especially bones.

B. Special machines are necessary for man to produce the mechanical stress needed for healthy bones.

C. Gravity on Earth provides sufficient mechanical stress for humans to maintain healthy bones.

D. Unmanned spacecrafts also need a lot of mechanical stress to fly out of the solar system.

4. Which is true regarding impact load?

A. In space, bones do not need an impact load to keep them healthy, thanks to weightlessness.

B. The impact loads that people experience in sport cause mechanical stress and strengthen bones.

C. The higher bone density becomes, the more impact load athletes experience.

D. Painful sports, such as judo or rugby, cause too much impact load to maintain healthy bones.

5. What is the author's claim?

A. Those who experience weightlessness suffer from a disease called osteoporosis.

B. Nowadays, more and more young people suffer from osteoporosis than before.

C. Exercise with a strong impact load is necessary to achieve adequate bone density.

D. The environment in space is so different that we can hardly learn anything from it.

≫ Summary

E (　　) にあてはまる語句を語群から選んで入れて、本文の要約を完成させてください。

Man has not traveled (1.　　) the moon so far. One of the primary reasons is that it is very difficult to keep (2.　　) healthy in a weightless environment. In space, we cannot easily (3.　　) ourselves to sufficient mechanical stress, or impact load, which we are able to do on Earth due to (4.　　). On the ground, we continuously (5.　　) our bones with mechanical stress through activities, such as lifting, bending, or simply standing. We can further strengthen our bones by doing some (6.　　) with high impact loads, namely sports with (7.　　) and contact, such as judo or football. Also, we could avoid suffering from osteoporosis if we start doing (8.　　) exercise earlier in life. In sum, whether in space or on Earth, proper exercise is always an (9.　　) part of a healthy life.

✦ **語群**

a. beyond　b. bones　c. collisions　d. essential　e. exercise
f. expose　g. gravity　h. moderate　i. strengthen

≫ Writing Activities < 否定 negation>

F 日本語の意味になるように、(　　) 内の語句を並び替えましょう。

1. 私達は最近購入した家が欠陥住宅だとは夢にも思わなかった。
   Little (did / dream that / the house / was / we / we bought recently) faulty.

   ____

2. 過去 30 年間にこの町に起こった大きな変化は誰の目にも明らかであろう。
   (can / fail to / no / notice / of the / one / the great changes) town over the past 30 years.

   ____

3. 嵐のような天候により私達は最初の実験を開始することができなかった。
   (from / prevented / starting / stormy weather / the / us) first experiment.

   ____

G 日本語の意味になるように、(　　) 内に入る適切な語句を選びましょう。

1. 太郎にとってその選挙結果はとうてい納得のいくものではなかった。

   Taro was (　　　　　　) satisfied with the result of the election.

   a. at all cost　　b. by no means　　c. nevertheless　　d. no longer

2. ステージでの彼らの演奏は期待はずれなものだった。

   Their performance on the stage was (　　　　　) expected.

   a. by far　　b. far from　　c. free without　　d. free of

≫ Listening Activity 19

H Dictation ≫ Write what you hear.

1. ______________________________ beyond the moon due to the difficulty of maintaining bone health in space.

2. ________________________ how the human body loses calcium from bone tissue in a weightless situation.

3. *Osteoporosis* is a disease in which bone ______________________ ________ from bone tissue and is likely to crack or break.

4. In order to live a happier life, ____________________________ mechanical stress is recommended for everyone.

≫ Another Challenge

I 私達が健康的な生活をおくる上でスポーツが果たす役割や効能について広く調べてみましょう。

Unit 10 Child Maltreatment

児童虐待

⋙ Warm-up Activities

A 下記の質問について話し合ってみましょう。

1. Do you know how many children are abused every year in Japan?
2. What do you think are the reasons why child maltreatment has not gone away?
3. What are the keys to recognizing child maltreatment?

B 下記の語句に該当する日本語を右から選び、その記号を（　）に書き入れましょう。

1. (　　) biological
2. (　　) fatal
3. (　　) fiscal year
4. (　　) psychological
5. (　　) adversely
6. (　　) omit
7. (　　) critical
8. (　　) superficial

(a) 表面の、表面的な
(b) 心理学の、 心理的な
(c) 逆に; 悪く、不都合に
(d) 生物学的な、血のつながった
(e) 除外する、…するのを怠る
(f) 致死的な
(g) 会計年度
(h) 重大な

C Bに出てきた語句を（　）に入れて文を完成させてください。必要な場合は形を変えてください。

1. An accurate grasp of risk is (　　　　　　　　　　) to the future of our company.

2. Her health was (   ) affected by the climate of the region.
3. People often (   ) necessary commas, which alters the meaning of the sentence.
4. The sunlight tells your body's (   ) clock that it's time to wake up.
5. This (   ) car accident is still under investigation.

Child Maltreatment [20]

You might think that child maltreatment is only caused by mentally deranged parents or only occurs in abnormal families. You may also have an image that stepmothers or stepfathers are more likely to abuse their stepchildren than their biological parents. However, neither of these are true. Child maltreatment may occur in any family, and in most cases, the perpetrators are the child's parents. In fact, among the fatal cases from 2003 to 2019, more than half of the perpetrators were the biological mothers.

1. ____________________ 児童虐待
2. ______________ 錯乱の、発狂した
3. ______________ 犯人、加害者

In Japan, child maltreatment is a serious social problem. The number of cases handled at child guidance centers has continued to increase for more than 30 years and reached approximately 190,000 nationwide in the 2019 fiscal year. In the 2018 fiscal year, 73 children died because of maltreatment, with some cases being a direct result from the parents.

4. ______________ 深刻な
5. ____________________ 児童相談所
6. ______________ おおよそ
7. ______________ 親

There are four types of child maltreatment: physical, sexual, psychological, and neglect, which often cause delayed growth and impaired physical and mental development, and can adversely affect the psychological well-being of a child. The four types of maltreatment are defined as follows:

8. ______________ 放置
9. ______________ 損なう
10. ______________ 次の通り

❇ Physical Abuse: Assaulting a child in a manner that will cause or is likely to cause injury to the child's body.

❇ Sexual Abuse: Engaging in sexual acts with a child or forcing a child to engage in those acts.

❇ Psychological Abuse: Inflicting emotional harm through words or actions, such as scolding a child through yelling or screaming. In addition, a child's exposure to violence between his/her parents is considered to be psychological abuse, as well as when words or actions of caring are omitted or withheld.

❇ Neglect: Failing to provide for or meet a child's basic physical, emotional, educational, and medical needs.

There are multiple risk factors that may lead to child maltreatment. Social isolation of the primary caregiver is one of the most critical risk factors. For example, a couple who had lived in Osaka moved to Tokyo for business just after the birth of their first baby. The child's mother took care of the baby by herself at their apartment all day while the father was busy at work until late at night. In her new home, she did not have any close friends or family to help her. She experienced feelings of anxiety and loneliness to such a degree that when the baby did not sleep, eat, or stop crying, the mother's emotional stress was no longer manageable, and she yelled at and slapped her child.

In urban societies, relationships among neighbors tend to be superficial, and some parents have difficulty seeking help in their communities. Therefore, we must understand that child maltreatment could occur in any family, and we

11. ____________ 危害を与える

12. ____________ 従事する

13. ____________ （苦痛などを）与える

14. ____________ 身をさらすこと

15. ____________ ～を与えずにおく

16. ____________ ～するのを怠る

17. ____________ 多様な

18. ____________ 非常に、大いに

19. ____________ 扱いやすい

20. ____________ 平手打ちする

need to watch over childrearing parents while building relationships with them. We all have to work together to combat child maltreatment, a social problem that may threaten our future.

(479 words)

21. ____________ 育児中、子育て

22. ____________ 立ち向かう

23. ____________ 脅かす

≫ Comprehension Check

D 内容に関する文を完成させるために、最も適切なものを選んでください。

1. What is true about child maltreatment?

A. Children are maltreated only when their parents are mentally disturbed.

B. Most of the victims are children who were mistreated by their stepparents.

C. Maltreated children will never be delayed in mental and physical development.

D. Studies show that in more than half of all fatal cases, children are maltreated by their own biological parents.

2. Cases of child maltreatment ______.

A. have dropped sharply for the past three decades

B. jumped in the year of 2019

C. have been growing over the last three decades

D. have been at the same level

3. When children are not provided with their basic physical, emotional, educational, and medical needs, it is regarded as ______.

A. physical abuse

B. sexual abuse

C. psychological abuse

D. neglect

4. What kind of situation is mentioned that could result in maltreatment?

A. Mothers feel so lonely when they take care of their children all alone.

B. Mothers cannot ask for help to look after their children.

C. Mothers cannot control their feelings when they are stressed out.

D. All of the above

5. According to the author, how should our society tackle the problem of child maltreatment?

A. Younger parents should live close to their family to ask for help.

B. Local communities should build a close relationship with childrearing parents.

C. Companies should create a more comfortable working environment for working mothers.

D. The government should provide subsidies for couples with small children.

≫ Summary

E (　)にあてはまる語句を語群から選んで入れて、本文の要約を完成させてください。

We should understand that child maltreatment could (1.　　) in any family. As a matter of fact, children are often maltreated by their (2.　　) parents. The number of reported cases has been on the (3.　　) over the last three decades, and the mental and (4.　　) development of those children could be (5.　　). There are four types of maltreatment, such as physical, sexual, psychological (6.　　), and neglect. One of the risk factors causing maltreatment is social (7.　　) caregivers are faced with when they bring up children. It is important for local (8.　　) to provide help for parents and build closer (9.　　) with them to handle the problem.

✦ **語群**

a. rise	b. hindered	c. communities	d. happen	e. abuse
f. ties	g. biological	h. physical	i. isolation	

⋙ Writing Activities < 分詞 particles>

F 日本語の意味になるように、(　　) 内の語句を並び替えましょう。

1. 私たちは 2 時間近く待たされた。
   They (for / kept / two / almost / waiting / us / hours).
   ____

2. テキストを小脇に抱えているのがホー先生です。
   The man (under / some / Mr. Haugh / arm / textbooks / his / is / holding).
   ____

3. 彼女はその知らせを聞いてとても驚いているようだった。
   She (the / very / to / surprised / hear / looked / news).
   ____

G 次の文を分詞構文を使って書き換えましょう。

1. When he arrived at the station, Sam found that the train had already left.
   ____

2. Since I didn’t know what to say, I was just sitting beside her.
   ____

⋙ Listening Activity 21

H Dictation ⋙ Write what you hear.

1. ______________________________, it is regarded as neglect.

2. If you find ______________________, you should report it to a child guidance center.

3. We should not yell or scream at children ______________________.

4. Mothers feel isolated in a small apartment and are often overwhelmed ______________________.

≫ Another Challenge

I 海外における児童虐待への取り組みについて調べ、グループで話し合ってみましょう。

✍

Unit 11 SDGs

持続可能な開発目標

⋙ Warm-up Activities

A 下記の質問について話し合ってみましょう。

1. What does SDGs stand for?
2. Which of all the SDGs are you most interested in?
3. What can you do to achieve SDGs in your daily life?

B 下記の語句に該当する日本語を右から選び、その記号を（　）に書き入れましょう。

1. (　　) admiration
2. (　　) lifelong
3. (　　) aspect
4. (　　) philanthropy
5. (　　) aftermath
6. (　　) emphasize
7. (　　) strive
8. (　　) feasible

(a) 博愛、慈善行為
(b) …を強調する、重要視する
(c) 生涯続く、終生の
(d) 実行できる、実現可能な
(e) （災害・戦争などの）余波
(f) 賞賛
(g) 努力する、励む
(h) 外観、様子、局面

C Bに出てきた語句を（　）に入れて文を完成させてください。必要な場合は形を変えてください。

1. Researchers have (　　　　　　　　　　) to understand the evolution of life on Earth.
2. The country should improve (　　　　　　　　　　) learning systems.

3. The mayor expressed his gratitude to all the volunteers who helped in the (　　　　　　　) of the torrential rain.
4. It needs to be shown that the plan is technically (　　　　　　　).
5. We can't take action until we understand all (　　　　　　　) of the problem.

22

Japanese For-Profit Companies as Agents of Social Change

Following the end of World War II, the Japanese economy grew mainly as its manufacturing industry developed. Japanese products won admiration from all over the world because they were safe and of high quality. Japanese companies also played a growing role in the social welfare of Japanese citizens, guaranteeing lifelong employment and benefits that are typically only provided in other countries by government-run social safety net programs. Although lifelong employment has largely disappeared in the last two decades, Japanese corporations are now contributing very broadly to society in new, and perhaps even more impactful ways.

1. ______________ 保証する
2. ______________ 終身雇用
3. ______________ 社会的セーフティネット
4. ______________ 影響力のある

The way companies contribute in society can be seen not only in Japan but also in other countries around the world. These days, nonprofit organizations (NPOs) are not the only ones to <u>address</u> social issues, such as poverty, environmental affairs, and elderly care issues. Many companies engaged in the manufacturing and service industries are trying to solve social issues through the lens of corporate social responsibility (CSR), a concept that primarily advocates for patronage and philanthropy, by developing new businesses. As companies, they support cultural and artistic activities to contribute to society.

5. ______________ 製造
6. ______________ 主として
7. ______________ 支援

Suntory, for instance, has established three public-interest incorporated foundations to contribute to the development of the arts, culture, and academics. The Suntory Museum of Art opened in 1961, and the Suntory Hall opened in 1986 as the first hall specifically designed for classical music in Tokyo. In addition, by establishing the Suntory Foundation for Life Sciences Bioorganic Research Institute to improve people's health and nutrition, Suntory has produced researchers who are active on the front lines of their research fields. At the same time, All Nippon Airways (ANA) and Yamato Transport Corporation have focused on philanthropy, providing voluntary transport of emergency relief supplies to afflicted areas in the aftermath of natural disasters, such as heavy rains or earthquakes.

8. ________________ 特に

9. ________________ 緊急救援物資

10. ________________ 災害地

Furthermore, in recent years, Japanese companies have emphasized Sustainable Development Goals (SDGs), which list seventeen goals that members of the United Nations should achieve by 2030. Some of the goals include no poverty, good health and well-being, and sustainable cities and communities. Many companies have been striving to achieve these goals through their business. Toyota Motor Corporation (TOYOTA), a leading Japanese company, is also contributing to their own SDGs. They develop electric vehicles (EV) and fuel cell vehicles (FCV) to reduce CO_2 emissions, and they participate in several projects to conserve global ecosystems, thus helping the world address environmental issues with a combination of their technology and corporate influence.

11. ________________ 達成する

12. ________________ 放射、排出

13. ________________ 保護する

In conclusion, social contributions from companies will be valuable for our future. However, it is neither easy nor feasible to achieve the seventeen SDGs only through the efforts of individual companies. Therefore, building networks of companies and NPOs to collaborate may be essential in the future.

(460 words)

≫ Comprehension Check

D 内容に関する文を完成させるために、最も適切なものを選んでください。

1. The following sentences are true about Japanese companies except _______.

A. Japanese companies grew rapidly in the postwar period

B. Japanese companies have been highly commended for their quality of goods

C. Japanese companies adopted lifetime employment schemes and provided benefits for their workers

D. Japanese companies have paid less attention to contributing to society recently

2. Choose a sentence in which the word "address" is used in the same way as underlined in the second paragraph.

A. The envelope was correctly addressed, but it didn't reach him.

B. Many companies failed to address the problem.

C. You should address the judge as Your Honor.

D. The presidential candidate addressed the visiting delegates.

3. Choose a correct combination of the name of the company and their social engagement activity.

A. Suntory -They provided financial support to young musicians.

B. ANA -They opened an art museum and a concert hall.

C. Yamato Transport Corporation -They delivered relief supplies to disaster-stricken areas.

D. TOYOTA -They founded a research institute to promote health and nutrition.

4. Which is true about the SDGs?

A. They were primarily set to promote good health to people around the world.

B. They focus on narrowing the gap between the rich and the poor.

C. They are targeted on auto companies, such as TOYOTA.

D. They are supported by many companies from different industries.

5. Which sentence best describes the author's idea?

A. There is no need for each person to make efforts to achieve the seventeen goals.

B. Each company should engage in achieving the seventeen goals.

C. Businesses and NPOs should cooperate with each other in achieving the seventeen goals.

D. NPOs should make more efforts to achieve the seventeen goals.

≫ Summary

E (　)にあてはまる語句を語群から選んで入れて、本文の要約を完成させてください。

Nowadays, many companies in Japan are trying to contribute to society in (1.　　) ways. One manufacturer engages in promoting art, as well as (2.　　) a research institute to improve our health and (3.　　). Some other companies in the (4.　　) industry are offering (5.　　) delivery of relief supplies to (6.　　) areas. There is another example of an (7.　　) that established its own SDGs to (8.　　) greenhouse gasses and has exerted a great (9.　　) on preserving our ecosystem. These social engagement activities are helpful to create a better society, but it will be necessary for these companies to (10.　　) together with NPOs to fully achieve the seventeen SDGs.

✦ **語群**

a. transport　b. auto maker　c. nutrition　d. work　e. disaster-stricken
f. reduce　g. founding　h. influence　i. free　j. broader

≫ Writing Activities < 能動態・受動態 active/possive voice>

F 次の英文を受動態の文に変えましょう。

1. What do you call this dish in French?

   ____?

2. They chose Sam as the captain of the team.

   ____.

3. My mother took care of the cats during our trip to New York.

   ____.

G 日本語の意味になるように、(　　) 内の語句を並び替えましょう。

1. 容疑者は現場から逃走するのを目撃された。

   The suspect (from / running / the / was / away / scene / seen).

   ____

2. 父は先週、自動車事故でけがをした。

   My father (last / was / in / car / a / week / accident / injured).

   ____

≫ Listening Activity 23

H Dictation ≫ Write what you hear.

1. Japanese companies have stressed the need to contribute to society, ____.

2. ______________________________________ have addressed social issues, such as poverty or environmental problems.

3. ______________________________________ has promoted electric vehicles and fuel cell vehicles to slash carbon emissions.

4. It will be necessary for Japanese companies ____________________ ____________________ to accomplish the seventeen goals of SDGs.

⋙ Another Challenge

I 日本企業の SDGs への取り組みについてさらに詳しく調べてみましょう。

✍

Unit 12 Adapted Sports

アダプテッド・スポーツ

≫ Warm-up Activities

A 下記の質問について話し合ってみましょう。

1. Do you know what sports were featured in the 2020 Summer Paralympics?
2. What do you think is the greatest danger for the visually impaired?
3. How can we contribute to the spread of sports for people with disabilities?

B 下記の語句に該当する日本語を右から選び、その記号を (　) に書き入れましょう。

1. (　　) adapt
2. (　　) disability
3. (　　) determine
4. (　　) inclusive
5. (　　) compete
6. (　　) outfit
7. (　　) guarantee
8. (　　) pursue

(a) 決定する
(b) 包括的、～を含んで
(c) 競う
(d) 装備する
(e) 追い求める
(f) 障がい
(g) 調整する
(h) 保証する

C Bに出てきた語句を (　) に入れて文を完成させてください。必要な場合は形を変えてください。

1. Good education does not always (　　　　　　　　) success in job hunting.

2. The two candidates were (   ) for the last remaining seat.
3. When the environment changes, it is necessary to (   ) our lifestyle to it.
4. The newly introduced game will be enjoyed by people with physical as well as mental (   ).
5. People tend to (   ) your value by the outcome, not by the effort you have made.

Adapting Sports for People with Disabilities 24

Sports for the disabled, with the Paralympic Games being the most well-known example, began as a result of reintroducing sports as part of the rehabilitation process for soldiers injured in World War II. Today, these sports are highly competitive, and athletes with different types and degrees of disability compete. Unlike general sports, which tend to exclude people based on height or physical size, sports for people with disabilities have devised rules, technologies, and concepts to make them more inclusive, while still accounting for a wide range of possible disabilities.

First, we need to examine the word "disability." The word itself does not tell us what part of the body is disabled, nor what kind of disability the person has, such as the difference between wheelchair users and amputees. Also, even for people who are visually impaired, the degree of vision varies from person to person, from those who cannot see at all to those who can see vague shapes and colors. Even though these people enjoy sports like the rest of us, sports authorities must consider each disability and make accommodations for things that a person would be unable to do due to their disability. Otherwise, their disabilities may determine their superiority or inferiority even before the game begins.

1. ________________ 障がい者
2. ________________ 再導入
3. ________________ 競い合っている
4. ________________ 除外する
5. ________________ 工夫する
6. ________________ 包括的
7. ________________ 考慮して
8. ________________ 切断手術を受けた人
9. ________________ 便宜
10. ________________ 決める
11. ________________ 優位
12. ________________ 劣位

Therefore, two concepts have been created for athletes with disabilities. The first is to devise tools and rules, and the second is to divide disabilities and compete fairly. Let's take wheelchair basketball, which is regarded as a star competition among people with disabilities, as an example.

13. ________________ 分ける

First, to devise tools and rules, wheelchair basketball does not have a double-dribble rule so that athletes can better control the ball while operating a wheelchair. Furthermore, wheelchairs used in competitions are different from those used in daily life. Wheelchair basketball uses light and highly mobile competitive wheelchairs, outfitted with rear wheels which have the shape of the Chinese character for eight.

14. ________________ 操作
15. ________________ 機動性の
16. ________________ 装備された
17. ________________________ 漢字

Regarding the second concept, to divide disabilities and compete fairly, in wheelchair basketball, the five players who participate in the game are given a point between 1.0 and 4.5 before the game begins depending on the degree of their disabilities. The players with the most severe disabilities will be given one point, while the players with the mildest disabilities will be given 4.5 points, and the total of the five players should be 14.0 points or less. This guarantees the opportunity for players with severe disabilities to participate in the games fairly.

18. ________________ 参加する
19. ________________ 保証する

Sports for people with disabilities with such ingenuity are called adapted sports. As the name implies, adapted sports means sports that flexibly apply new tools or rules to adapt to the physical and mental condition of the person according to the type and degree of disability. On the other hand, traditional sports have pursued efficiency and excellence by training people and adapting to existing tools and rules. However, in such a

20. ________________ 創意工夫
21. ________________________ （暗に）意味を持つ
22. ________________ 柔軟に
23. ________________ 追求した
24. ________________ 効率
25. ________________ 既存の

traditional way, there are people who cannot participate in sports and are left behind.

It is the idea of adapted sports that has supported the development of sports for people with disabilities today. In order to improve the quality of human life and society, it is necessary for those without disabilities to be more aware of the difficulties faced by people with disabilities. Instead of asking people with disabilities to solve the difficulties they face in society, we should all realize that society may be responsible for those difficulties and think about what we can do as a society and act accordingly. With just one apostrophe, the meaning changes from "Impossible" to "I'm possible." In this way, a small effort by each person can change society for the better. (609 words)

26. ______________ 置き去りになる

27. ______________ 健常者

28. __________ 解決する

29. __________ 適宜に

⋙ Comprehension Check

D 内容に関する文を完成させるために、最も適切なものを選んでください。

1. According to the passage, ______.

A. a part of the rehabilitation process for injured soldiers was to make them compete in mental games

B. the rules of sports reintroduced for rehabilitation purposes were more inclusive than those of general sports

C. sports were introduced to the soldiers in order to keep them under control

D. athletes injured in World War II began to revise the rules of general sports to make them more competitive

2. The word "disabled" ______.

A. tells us that the person concerned is either a wheelchair user or an amputee

B. does not tell us what part of the body is disabled

C. is used to show that a certain function is totally missing

D. is not used to indicate any lack of mental ability

3. Wheelchair basketball ______.

A. is irrelevant to adapted sports

B. is a game for players in wheelchairs with the Chinese character for eight

C. can be played by athletes with different levels of disability

D. is played under the same rules as normal athletes

4. Unlike adapted sports, traditional sports ______.

A. have pursued excellent performances by trained players

B. have been under unchangeable rules

C. are so competitive that normal people are unable to play

D. are not flexible to apply new tools or rules

5. According to the author, ______.

A. adapted sports have supported the development of sports for the disabled

B. only a small change in society can improve effort from everybody

C. our society is not aware of difficulties faced by those with disabilities

D. it is impossible for those with disabilities to improve the rules of sports

≫ Summary

E (　　) にあてはまる語句を語群から選んで入れて、本文の要約を完成させてください。

Unlike general sports, adapted sports, or sports for the (1.　　), have devised (2.　　), (3.　　), and (4.　　) to make them more (5.　　). Adapted sports have flexibly applied new tools or rules to adapt to the (6.　　) and (7.　　) condition of the participant according to the type and degree of disability. Dividing disabilities (8.　　) the opportunity for players with different disabilities to (9.　　) in the games fairly. Adapted sports have supported the development of sports for people with disabilities. To improve the (10.　　) of human life and society, those (11.　　) disabilities must be more (12.　　) of the difficulties that people with disabilities face.

✦ 語群

a. aware	b. concepts	c. disabled	d. guarantees	e. inclusive
f. mental	g. participate	h. physical	i. quality	j. rules
k. technologies	l. without			

⋙ Writing Activities <形容詞 adjective>

F 日本語の意味になるように、(　　) 内の語句を並び替えましょう。

1. キンバリーは古くてすり切れた袖をまくりあげ、霜の降りた堅くて黒い地面を掘り起こすつもりになっていました。
Kimberly was rolling (and / her / old / sleeves/ up / worn), ready to dig up (black / frosty / hard / the) ground.

2. 物がはっきり見えるくらい明るくなるまで外にでないでください。
Please stay (becomes / bright / indoors / it / until) so (are / clearly / that / things) visible.

3.「茶色の機敏な狐が怠惰な犬を跳び越える」はよく知られている書き方練習の文です。
"The (brown / dog / fox / jumps / lazy / over / quick / the)" is (a / for / handwriting / practice / sentence / used / well-known).

G 日本語の意味になるように (　　) 内に適切な語句を入れましょう。

1. その事故はタクシーと自転車双方に同じくらい責任があった。
Both the taxi driver and the cyclist (　　　　　　) (　　　　　　) (　　　　　　) for the accident.

2. 面白い本が読む価値があるとは限らない。
Interesting books are (　　　　　　) (　　　　　　) (　　　　　　) (　　　　　　).

3. どんな企業も環境保護に無関心であってはなりません。
No company should be (　　　　　　) (　　　　　　) (　　　　　　) protection.

≫ Listening Activity 25

H Dictation ≫ Write what you hear.

1. As I read the Articles of the Social Welfare Act, ____________________

   ____.

2. Though “I’m possible” ____

   ____

   __________ what it implies.

3. It is possible ____

   ____.

4. Boccia is ____

   ______________________________________.

≫ Another Challenge

I 日本では戦争で身体に障がいを負った兵士（傷痍軍人）のリハビリテーションにはどのような方策を講じたのか調べてみましょう。

Unit 13 Social Welfare Practice in Communities

地域における社会福祉実践

⋙ Warm-up Activities

A 下記の質問について話し合ってみましょう。

1. Have you ever heard of the declining birthrate, aging society, shrinking families, and the disparity in wealth?
2. Are these changes happening around you?
3. Do you think these changes will affect your life?

B 下記の語句に該当する日本語を右から選び、その記号を（　）に書き入れましょう。

1. (　　) disparity
2. (　　) autonomous
3. (　　) provision
4. (　　) comprehensive
5. (　　) exclusion
6. (　　) compensation
7. (　　) infrastructure
8. (　　) collaboration

(a) 提供・供給
(b) 共同（作業）・協力
(c) 補償
(d) 格差
(e) 基礎・土台
(f) 排除
(g) 総合的な
(h) 自律的な

C Bに出てきた語句を（　）に入れて文を完成させてください。必要な場合は形を変えてください。

1. My father received $4,000 in (　　　　　　　) from the insurance company for injuries caused by a traffic accident.

2. At the request of the citizens for alternative energy sources, the mayor decided to make a plan to produce renewable energy in ( ) with environmental scientists.
3. A newly elected congresswoman pointed out that there is a big ( ) between the rate of pay for men and women in this country.
4. In Spain, there are some ( ) regions where they can shape policy and govern themselves.
5. After the earthquake, when thousands of people sought shelter at the city hall, the food ( ) ran out in a short time.

Social Welfare Practice in Communities 26

Social welfare practice aims to be given within the community or as close to the community as possible. This is because a person's existence is recognized in the context of social relationships, in which self-actualization is established through the engagement of roles. However, nowadays in Japan, rapid changes in social structure, such as the declining birthrate, aging society, shrinking families, and the disparity in wealth, are hindering social welfare aims. For example, our rapidly aging society is leading to social issues such as the isolation of older people living alone. At the same time, we are faced with a critical shortage of caregivers needed to support the livelihood of the elderly. In Japan, the goal of social welfare is to solve these problems through community welfare, which involves two types of practices.

The first is to support people's daily lives so that everyone can achieve self-fulfillment in familiar surroundings, no matter what their disabilities might be. This is called community care. This kind of care requires multidisciplinary professionals to cooperate and work together as a team. In general, residential facilities provide services that support residents' lives 24/7 and are mostly autonomous.

1. ________________ ～の関係において
2. ________________ 自己実現
3. ________________ 関与
4. ________________ 家族の縮小
5. ________________ 妨げる
6. ________________ 暮らし
7. ________________ 自己達成
8. ________________ 多くの専門分野にわたる
9. ________________ 居住型施設
10. ________________ 年中無休

Therefore, the services are efficient, but the facility tends to be enclosed in its own circumstances. On the other hand, in a local community, numerous services are active independently, so service providers need to cooperate with them. This system is called care management. Furthermore, the provision of services focusing on welfare, nursing care, health care, and medical care is called comprehensive care. In recent years, there has been an increasing demand for broad cooperation in all aspects of life-related services that had previously been provided by family members.

11. ______________ 効率的な
12. ______________ 施設
13. ______________ 傾向がある

The second practice is the creation of communities where healthy human relationships can be formed without exclusion or isolation. To achieve this, it is necessary to promote human rights education and volunteer activities to raise awareness of the residents' welfare. These efforts will ultimately result in the early detection and treatment of those who need assistance. This is considered to be the goal of community care as community care by the community.

14. ______________ 結局は
15. ______________ 発覚

For people loneliness is a personal emotion that occurs in the process of the development of the personality. Furthermore, solitude is a more severe emotion, but this emotion also makes one grow as a person. However, solitude is also a social problem if it arises from a situation in which one cannot connect with another. This is called social isolation. Social isolation is a harsh situation that denies a human being the experience of social relations. Japan is a country with a high degree of people suffering from loneliness relative to other developed countries. It has also been pointed out that social isolation and poverty are closely related. Therefore, social welfare and social security have come to include some measures to improve isolation issues. These measures

16. ______________ 孤独
17. ______________ 過酷な

function as a safety net, including specific income compensation and community care.

In the next 20 years, it is predicted that Japan's social structure will change drastically due to the falling birthrate and the aging and shrinking population, so some restructuring of the overall social welfare system to respond to these changes is needed. As one example, social welfare and social security need to be enhanced as a new form of supportive infrastructure and support.

18. ______________ 激烈に

To sum up, social welfare is a practice and policy that aims to achieve wellbeing and enrich peoples' lives, as well as provide a safety net for one's life. It is required in order to create a community where people are not isolated. Furthermore, community welfare promotes comprehensive community care through the collaboration of residents, who individually form their own lives as members of the community. This has become the mainstream of social welfare in Japan today. (629 words)

19. ______________ 要約すると

20. ______________ 豊かにする

⋙ Comprehension Check

D 内容に関する文を完成させるために、最も適切なものを選んでください。

1. Why is it necessary to provide social welfare programs within the community or as close to the community as possible?

A. Because rapid changes in social structure, such as the declining birthrate, are hindering social welfare aims.

B. Because a person's existence is recognized in the context of social relationships.

C. Because in recent years, there has been an increasing demand for broad cooperation in all aspects of our lives.

D. Because in a local community, numerous services are active independently.

2. Other than a declining birthrate and aging society, which of the following is hindering social welfare aims?

A. Shrinking families and the disparity in wealth

B. A critical shortage of caregivers

C. The isolation of older people living alone

D. Community care

3. How can we solve a critical shortage of caregivers?

A. By promoting human rights education

B. By the early detection and treatment of those who need assistance

C. By specific income compensation

D. By shifting from residential-type facilities to "community care by the community"

4. Although solitude is sometimes necessary to make one grow as a person, social isolation is said not to be a desirable situation. Why is it not so desirable?

A. Because it denies a human being the experience of social relations.

B. Because Japan is a country with a high degree of people suffering from loneliness.

C. Because social welfare and social security are closely related.

D. Because it functions as a safety net.

5. What is the mainstream of social welfare in Japan?

A. Services provided by family members

B. Residential facilities where services are provided 24 hours a day

C. Community care through the collaboration of multidisciplinary professionals and residents

D. Self-support without any support from the government

≫ Summary

E (　)にあてはまる語句を語群から選んで入れて、本文の要約を完成させてください。

Nowadays in Japan, the birthrate is declining, the society is (1.　　), (2.　　) are shrinking, and the (3.　　) is growing, and these changes are affecting Japan's social structure. For instance, the number of senior citizens living alone is increasing and yet they cannot receive the care which had been previously provided by their (4.　　). The number of families who need financial support is also increasing, so, many more social welfare providers will be necessary. Yet we are faced with a critical shortage of (5.　　). In the next 20 years, it is predicted that Japan's social structure will change drastically, and restructuring of the social welfare system is needed. This new system has been developing, and is called (6.　　). It is becoming the (7.　　) of social welfare in Japan. Instead of providing residential-type facilities (8.　　), people receive necessary care where they live. In this system, care givers work together with multidisciplinary professionals as (9.　　). Together with them, community care also asks the (10.　　) to participate in the community. In this way, the collaboration of professionals and residents is allowing comprehensive community care to become the mainstream of social welfare in Japan.

✦ **語群**

a. mainstream　b. caregivers　c. family members　d. 24 hours a day
e. a team　f. family sizes　g. residents　h. aging
i. disparity in wealth　j. community care by the community

≫ Writing Activities < 仮定法 subjunctive>

F 以下の英文中の ( ) 内の選択肢から正しいものを選びましょう。

1. I wish I (**a.** haven't cooked **b.** hadn't cooked) beef stew yesterday.
   I (**a.** don't know **b.** didn't know) he was a vegetarian.

2. If it (a. rain b. rains c. will rain) tomorrow, the excursion (**a.** is **b.** will be **c.** would be) postponed.

3. If Mary (**a.** had married **b.** would have married **c.** have married) him at that time, she would be a mother by now.

G 日本語の意味になるように、(　　) 内に適切な語句を入れましょう。

1. 私だったら英語の授業をサボらないわ。
   If I (　　　　　) you, I (　　　　　) (　　　　　) skip English class.

2. メアリーは医者の仕事楽しくないのよ。女優だったら良いのにと思っているのよ。
   Mary doesn't enjoy being a doctor. She (　　　　　) she (　　　　　) an actress.

3. もう一度チャンスがあれば良いのだが。
   If only I (　　　　　) another (　　　　　).

≫ Listening Activity 27

H Dictation ≫ Write what you hear.

1. Social welfare aims ____
   ________________________.

2. This kind of care requires multidisciplinary __________________
   ____ as a team.

3. Social isolation is a harsh situation that ______________________
   __________________________.

4. To sum up, social welfare is a practice and policy that ______________
   ________________________________, as well as provide a safety net for one's life.

≫ Another Challenge

I 大都市と地方都市などの地域によって介護制度に違いがあるのか調べてみましょう。

Unit 14

COMSi: An Example of Social Enterprise in Japan

こむの事業所

≫ Warm-up Activities

A 下記の質問について話し合ってみましょう。

1. How do social enterprises differ from volunteering and charities?
2. Do you know of any specific social enterprises? What are they?
3. What influence do social enterprises have on our society?

B 下記の語句に該当する日本語を右から選び、その記号を（　）に書き入れましょう。

1. (　　) disadvantage
2. (　　) continuous
3. (　　) significant
4. (　　) contribute
5. (　　) lead to
6. (　　) exclude
7. (　　) guarantee
8. (　　) acknowledge

(a) 貢献する
(b) ～に至る、～につながる
(c) 保証する
(d) 排除する
(e) 継続的な
(f) 認める
(g) 不利、不都合
(h) 重要な、重大な、かなりの

C Bに出てきた語句を（　　）に入れて文を完成させてください。必要な場合は形を変えてください。

1. Lack of sleep (　　　　　　　　　　) trouble with thinking and concentration.
2. A (　　　　　　　　　　) number of people work at social enterprises in Europe.

3. He didn't ( ) our efforts to make our working environment comfortable.
4. We should not ( ) socially vulnerable people from our community.
5. The company always ( ) the high quality of its products.

COMSi: An Example of Social Enterprise in Japan 28

In recent years, there has been a strong interest in work integration social enterprises[1]. These are social enterprises that provide workplaces for people with disabilities or who are facing other disadvantages that make it difficult to find employment in the general labor market. While particularly popular in European countries, social enterprises are present in some form worldwide, including Japan. First, let's look at how social enterprises are defined in Europe.

The Emergence of Social Enterprise in Europe (EMES) project, conducted by the European Commission, defines social enterprises as having both economic and social aspects. According to Borzoga and Defourny (2001)[2], there are four economic standards: a continuous activity producing goods and/or selling services, a high degree of autonomy, a significant level of economic risk (for those who establish social enterprises), and a minimum level of paid workers. At the same time, there are also the following five social standards for social enterprises: it must be an organization established by citizens, have a clear purpose of contributing to the community, make decisions that are not based on capital ownership, allow participation for all of those involved, and limit profit distribution. Therefore, social enterprises in Europe are defined by these nine items that combine economic and social standards.

1. ______ 障害
2. ______ 雇用
3. ______ 労働市場
4. ______ 定義する
5. ______ 行う
6. ______ 側面
7. ______ 程度、度合い
8. ______ 自立性
9. ______ 設立する
10. ______ 最小の
11. ______ 利潤分配
12. ______ 合わせる

Also, the main areas of European social enterprises are labor integration and (personal) social services that are closely linked to the local community. Within these two areas, a social enterprise that aims at labor integration is considered to be a social firm. As the number of social firms increases, so do employment opportunities for those at a social disadvantage. This in turn leads to greater social inclusion[3] for those who have somehow fallen through the cracks of society or have been unable to enter into the general workforce.

13. ______________ 目的とする

14. ______________ 社会的包摂

Here in Japan, social firms also have a presence. One example is an NPO called COMSi[4] in Takarazuka City, Hyogo Prefecture. COMSi is an NPO whose mission is to "create a community where no one is excluded." In order to carry out this mission, operating under the same laws and systems as other businesses in Japan, COMSi guarantees a minimum wage and provides employment opportunities for people with disabilities. In addition, COMSi actively employs not only people with disabilities but also those who struggle to get jobs in society, such as single parents, young people with withdrawal symptoms, and the elderly.

15. ______________ 存在感

16. ______________ 遂行する

17. ______________ 最低賃金

18. ______________ 苦闘する

19. ______________ ひきこもり

COMSi has four businesses: a cleaning business, a meal service business, a sales business, and a system development business. People with disabilities work and are active in all of these workplaces. Of course, there are situations where support is needed due to a disability, but it is important for the staff working there to cooperate with each other to carry out the work. In COMSi, various efforts are taken to create a comfortable working environment; for example, a work procedure is subdivided and transcribed into letters, visualized by using photographs, and so on.

20. ______________ 努力

21. ______________ 手順

22. ______________ 細分化する

23. ______________ 表記する

24. ______________ 視覚化する

Through businesses conducted at COMSi, those who work there are freed from discrimination and prejudice by understanding and acknowledging each other. In addition, by engaging with the local community through work, they can be recognized as a member of community. These efforts will realize the mission of COMSi business establishments, "creating a community where no one is excluded," and contribute to the social inclusion expectations of social enterprises.

(556 words)

25. ______________ 偏見

26. ______________________ 関わる

✦ **Notes / 注**

1. work integration social enterprise: 労働統合型社会的企業
2. Borzaga, C. & J. Defourny (Eds.). (2001). The Emergence of Social Enterprise. London: Routledge. (2004, 内山哲朗・石塚秀雄・柳澤敏勝訳 『社会的企業－雇用・福祉のサードセクター』 日本経済評論社)
3. social inclusion: 社会的包摂
4. COMSi: こむの事業所

⋙ Comprehension Check

D 内容に関する文を完成させるために、最も適切なものを選んでください。

1. What is inappropriate as a social standard to define social enterprise in Europe?

A. Social enterprises must have a clear objective of working to make the community better.

B. Social enterprises must prioritize capital ownership when they make decisions.

C. Social enterprises must allow all of those involved to participate in their business.

D. Social enterprises must be organizations founded by citizens.

2. What is NOT true about social firms?

A. They provide workplaces for people with disabilities.

B. Their goal is labor integration.

C. They employ people with disabilities but not young people with withdrawal symptoms.

D. The more social firms there are, the more easily socially weak people will be able to find employment opportunities.

3. What is NOT true about COMSi?

A. The four businesses of COMSi are a cleaning business, a meal service business, a sales business, and a human resource development business.

B. COMSi is a social firm that aims to create a community where no one is excluded.

C. COMSi is operating under the same laws and systems as other businesses in Japan.

D. In COMSi, a work procedure is subdivided and transcribed into letters, visualized by using photographs to create a comfortable working environment.

4. Why does the author mention COMSi?

A. Because the author wants to point out that social enterprises in Japan are behind Europe.

B. Because the author wants to compare social enterprises in Japan and those in Europe.

C. Because the author wants to introduce COMSi as a good example of a social firm in Japan.

D. Because the author wants to contribute to promoting regional development in Takarazuka.

5. Which of the following has nothing to do with COMSi's mission?

A. Employees at COMSi understand and recognize each other so that they do not feel discrimination or prejudice.

B. Those who work at COMSi will be recognized as a member of the community by engaging with the local community through work.

C. COMSi guarantees a minimum wage and provides employment opportunities for people with disabilities.

D. COMSi makes decisions that are based on capital ownership.

⋙ Summary

E (　　) にあてはまる語句を語群から選んで入れて、本文の要約を完成させてください。

Work (1.　　) social enterprises are (2.　　) attention in Europe. They are social enterprises that (3.　　) workplaces for people who have (4.　　) finding employment because of disabilities or other disadvantages. A social enterprise aiming at labor integration is considered a social firm. Social firms offer more employment opportunities for those at a social (5.　　), which (6.　　) to greater social inclusion. COMSi is a Japanese social firm whose mission is to "create a community where no one is (7.　　)." It employs not only people with disabilities but also people struggling to get a job and makes efforts to create a comfortable working environment. Businesses conducted at COMSi free people from (8.　　) and prejudice by mutual understanding, and help them be recognized as members of the community. These efforts will (9.　　) the mission of COMSi and (10.　　) to the social inclusion expectations for social enterprises.

✦ **語群**

a. realize　b. excluded　c. difficulties　d. leads
e. attracting　f. discrimination　g. contribute　h. integration
i. disadvantage　j. provide

⋙ Writing Activities < 関係副詞 relative adverbs>

F 日本語の意味になるように、(　　) 内の語句を並び替えましょう。

1. 誰も差別に苦しむことのないコミュニティを構築することが重要です。
(a community / is / build / discrimination / to / where /suffers / it / from / important / no one).

2. 私はその社会的企業がどのように設立されたのか知りたいです。
(to / how / the social enterprise / know / was / want / established / I).

3. これがソーシャル・ファームが増加している理由です。
(is / why / social firms / been / the reason / increasing / this /have).

G 次の 2 つの英文を、関係代名詞を使って 1 つの文にしてみましょう。

1. We need to create a workplace. Anyone can speak out there.

____

2. 2021 was the year. Tokyo 2020 Olympics was held in the year.

____

≫ Listening Activity 29

H Dictation ≫ Write what you hear.

1. Work integration social enterprises provide workplaces ________ ______________________________________ due to other disadvantages.

2. Providing more employment opportunities for people with social disadvantages ______________________________ __________.

3. When employees need support due to a disability, __________ ______________________________________.

4. Those who work at COMSi will be recognized as community members ____________________________________.

≫ Another Challenge

I Social enterprise について調べてみましょう。

Unit 15 Outdoor Education

野外教育

⋙ Warm-up Activities

A 下記の質問について話し合ってみましょう。

1. What do you think the person in the photographs is doing?
2. If you spend time outdoors, what do you like to do?
3. What kind of outdoor activities do you like?

B 下記の語句に該当する日本語を右から選び、その記号を（　）に書き入れましょう。

1. (　　) experiential
2. (　　) reflective
3. (　　) concrete
4. (　　) abstract
5. (　　) identify
6. (　　) modify
7. (　　) awareness
8. (　　) attitude

(a) 抽象的な
(b) 態度、考え方
(c) 内省的な、反映的な
(d) 修正する
(e) 気づき、認知、自覚
(f) 体験的な、経験に基づいた
(g) 具体的な
(h) (原因などを) 明らかにする、特定する

C Bに出てきた語句を（　　）に入れて文を完成させてください。必要な場合は形を変えてください。

1. Feedback and reflection can help to (　　　　　　　　　) potential problems.
2. After one year of trial, the school decided to (　　　　　　　　　) the program to make it more effective for their students.

3. We have (   ) evidence to arrest him for assault.
4. The main purpose of the organization is to raise (   ) about child poverty.
5. Examples of an (   ) concept include love, freedom, and sorrow.

Outdoor Education 30

Outdoor education is a method of instruction based on the more general theory of experiential education. If you asked people in a university class or even people on a camp-related seminar what outdoor education is, most would not know. However, most of them would be aware of the term experiential education, which uses the experiential learning cycle to promote learning by doing.

Doctor David Kolb and Doctor Alice Kolb proposed the experiential learning cycle, which consists of four stages and is outlined as follows: Stage 1 is the *concrete experience* stage where a learner has a new experience or undergoes a reinterpretation process of a previous experience. In the next stage, which is the *reflective observation* stage, the learner looks back and reexamines the new experience to identify any inconsistencies between experiences and their understanding. In Stage 3, the stage of *abstract conceptualization*, the process of reflection helps the learner form a new idea or concept or modify an existing abstract concept to form more generalized ideas. Finally, in the last stage, which is the *active experimentation* stage, the learner applies and tests the newly learned knowledge in new situations, and the learner once again restarts the four-stage cycle.

1. ________________ 指導法
2. ________________ 促進する
3. ________________ ～から成る
4. ________________ 再解釈
5. ________________ 以前の
6. ________________ 明らかにする
7. ________________ 矛盾
8. ________________ 内省
9. ________________ 概念
10. ________________ 修正する
11. ________________ 応用する

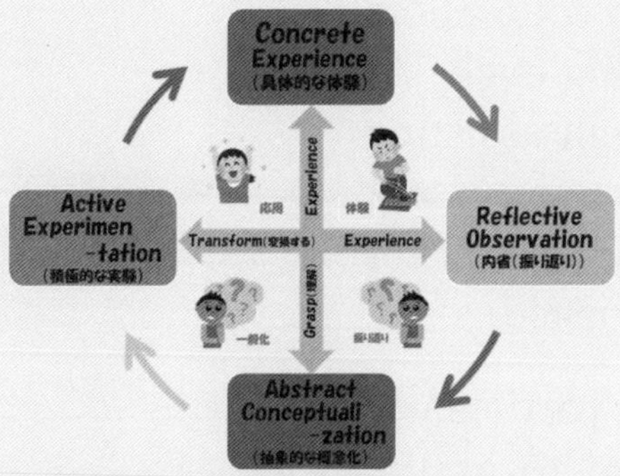

図1　The Experiential Learning Cycle (David A.KOLB)

Outdoor education uses outdoor activities as an experience in Stage 1 of the learning cycle. It is very important to use the learning cycle not only in experiential education but also in outdoor education. If the learning cycle is not used, then it will be just an outdoor activity without anything to learn from it.

Otto Friedrich Bollnow, who was a philosopher of education, wrote, “People often say that we encounter a lot of experiences in life, but most of them are meaningless facts. It will be an ‘experience’ only after you constantly assimilate and use your ‘awareness’ to decide your future attitude.”

12. ______________ 遭遇する
13. ______________ 無意味な
14. ______________ 同化する

For example, imagine an outdoor activity where you are tasked with trying to start a fire. If you are unable to start the fire, you might think it is difficult, and you may give up, which means that you are just having an experience and not learning anything from it. However, if you reflect on that experience and think about why it did not work and try it again, you may be able to learn something by being more aware of the situation. By using your awareness, you will be able to learn something from the experience. As you can see from this example, experiences are not only to be gained from outdoor education, but they are also a pathway to learning.

15. ______________ 任務を負う
16. ____________ ～を振り返る、顧みる
17. ____________ から得られる

College students who work as camp counsellors also support learners to use the learning cycle. At the same time, they also learn through assisting others. In other words, outdoor education is not only for learners, but can also be educational for everyone who is involved in the experience.

18. ______________ ～に携わる

Furthermore, outdoor education is particularly relevant today, in what is referred to as the era of VUCA. VUCA, an acronym that stands for Volatility, Uncertainty, Complexity, and Ambiguity, was first used in 1987 to describe today's world, which is more unpredictable than in earlier generations. VUCA can also describe the current situation surrounding us all at this moment. In a nutshell, it's an unpredictable state. As a result, each of us is required to live with a firm belief or opinion and make decisions without being influenced by those around us.

19. ______________ 関連のある

20. ______________ 頭文字

21. ______________ 変動性

22. ______________ 不確実性

23. ______________ 複雑性

24. ______________ 曖昧性

25. ______________ 予想不可能な

These days, many people are interested in outdoor education, such as Takeshi Okada, a former all-Japan soccer manager who used outdoor education with his team. When he was the manager of Hangzhou Ryokujo in the Chinese Super League, he brought his soccer players all the way from China to Japan to use outdoor education for team building. And he also opened his own outdoor education school, the Shimanami Outdoor School in Ehime prefecture, Japan. Other soccer players, such as top Japanese J-League players, youth players and junior youth players, have also been building strong teams through outdoor education.

A growing body of research is showing that outdoor education is a very effective tool for supporting reflective learning through experiences in the outdoors. I believe all educators could benefit by learning more about the potential of outdoor education as a method of education.

(705 words)

26. ______________ 恩恵を得る

27. ______________ 潜在力

≫ Comprehension Check

D 内容に関する文を完成させるために、最も適切なものを選んでください。

1. According to the passage, which of the following is NOT true for outdoor education?

A. Outdoor education is a teaching method based on experiential education.

B. In outdoor education, it is very important to use the learning cycle.

C. Outdoor education is educational for learners, but not for those who assist them.

D. Outdoor education is particularly relevant in the era of VUCA.

2. Which of the following is NOT true for the experiential learning cycle?

A. It was proposed by Doctor David Kolb and Doctor Alice Kolb in 2017.

B. It consists of four stages.

C. In its second stage, a learner has a new experience.

D. Its last stage involves applying newly learned knowledge in new situations.

3. Which of the following best describes Bollnow's idea about experiences mentioned in the fourth paragraph?

A. Experiences are meaningless facts unless people use their awareness for their future attitude.

B. People encounter a lot of meaningless experiences in life.

C. Otto Friedrich Bollnow was a philosopher of education with a lot of experiences.

D. People can decide their future attitude only after they assimilate their awareness.

4. What is the purpose of the fire starting example in the fifth paragraph?

A. If you fail to start a fire, you might just give up.

B. If you fail to start a fire and give up, it will still be a good experience.

C. If you think about why you fail and try again, you may learn something from the experience.

D. Experiences can be learned only from outdoor education.

5. What is being shown by research on outdoor education? Choose the best answer.

A. Outdoor education helps reflective learning through outdoor experiences.

B. Outdoor education is a very effective educational tool.

C. All teachers can be helped by learning about outdoor education.

D. All of the above

≫ Summary

E (　　) にあてはまる語句を語群から選んで入れて、本文の要約を完成させてください。

Outdoor education is a method of instruction based on the theory of experiential education, which uses an experiential leaning cycle. In this four-stage cycle, first you have a new experience, next (1.　　) on the experience, then form a new idea or (2.　　) an existing concept, and finally (3.　　) the newly learned knowledge in new situations. Experiences are the key factor in outdoor education and also a (4.　　) to learning. Today, in the cra of VUCA where things are (5.　　), outdoor education is particularly (6.　　) since we are required to have our own beliefs and make our own decisions. Both educators and learners can (7.　　) from outdoor education, so it has been used in many fields recently. Research shows outdoor education is a very effective educational (8.　　) for supporting (9.　　) learning.

✦ **語群**

a. benefit　b. apply　c. reflective　d. unpredictable
e. tool　f. reflect　g. relevant　h. modify
i. pathway

≫ Writing Activities <動名詞 gerund>

F 日本語の意味になるように、(　　) 内の語句を並び替えましょう。

1. 多くの人が週末屋外で過ごすことを楽しむ。
   (spending / people / many / enjoy / outdoors / time) on weekends.
2. 他の人を手伝うことを通して、あなたのスキルを向上できる。
   You can (skills / others / your / assisting / improve / through).
3. 経験を通して学ぶことが最も効果的な方法だ。
   (experience / is / through / leaning / most / the) effective way.

G 日本語の意味になるように、(　　) 内に適切な語を入れましょう。

1. 弁護士はついに被告人を擁護するのを諦めた。
   The lawyer finally (　　　　　) (　　　　　) defending the defendant.
2. 誰にも気づかれることなくその部屋を去った。
   I left the room without (　　　　　) (　　　　　) by anyone.

≫ Listening Activity 31

H Dictation ≫ Write what you hear.

1. Stage 1 is the *Concrete Experience* stage, where a learner has a new experience or undergoes ______________________________ __________.
2. ______________________________ __________ or modify an existing abstract concept to form more generalized ideas.
3. However, ______________________________ ________ and try it again, you may be able to learn something by being more aware of the situation.
4. As a result, each of us is required to live with a firm belief or opinion and make decisions ______________________________.

≫ Another Challenge

I 他にどのような場面で野外教育が実施されているか調べてみましょう。

Notes

Notes

Notes

Notes

作成者一覧（所属等は 2022 年度のもの）

<本文執筆・日本語試訳>

Unit 1　林眞帆　（関西学院大学人間福祉学部准教授）

Unit 2　澤田有希子（関西学院大学人間福祉学部准教授）

Unit 3　桜井智恵子（関西学院大学人間福祉学部教授）

Unit 4　村井琢哉　（関西学院大学人間福祉学部助教）

Unit 5　森重裕子　（関西学院大学人間福祉学部助教）

Unit 6　笹場育子　（立命館大学スポーツ健康科学部准教授）

Unit 7　風間朋子　（関西学院大学人間福祉学部准教授）

Unit 8　武田丈　（関西学院大学人間福祉学部教授）

Unit 9　河鰭一彦　（関西学院大学人間福祉学部教授）

Unit 10　馬場幸子　（関西学院大学人間福祉学部教授）

Unit 11　田原慎介　（公立諏訪東京理科大学共通・マネジメント教育センター講師）

Unit 12　中道莉央　（びわこ成蹊スポーツ大学生涯スポーツコース准教授）

Unit 13　藤井博志　（関西学院大学人間福祉学部教授）

Unit 14　平尾昌也　（関西学院大学人間福祉学部助教）

Unit 15　甲斐知彦　（関西学院大学人間福祉学部教授）

<設問作成、英文校閲、日本語試訳校閲>

Paul Aaloe（関西学院大学人間福祉学部非常勤講師）

Todd Allen（関西大学外国語学部准教授 / 関西学院大学人間福祉学部非常勤講師）

茨木正志郎（関西学院大学人間福祉学部准教授）

恵中あづさ（関西学院大学人間福祉学部非常勤講師）

小西貴子　（関西学院大学人間福祉学部非常勤講師）

小林亮哉　（関西学院大学人間福祉学部助教）

小林美智代（関西学院大学人間福祉学部非常勤講師）

Joe Jacobs（関西学院大学人間福祉学部非常勤講師）

武内祐樹　（関西学院大学人間福祉学部非常勤講師）

中野陽子　（関西学院大学人間福祉学部教授）

西村浩子　（周南公立大学福祉情報学部講師）

乗次章子　（関西学院大学人間福祉学部非常勤講師）

Sam Haugh（関西学院大学人間福祉学部英語常勤講師）

福居誠二　（関西学院大学人間福祉学部非常勤講師）

三浦秀松　（武庫川女子大学文学部教授）

山本路恵　（関西学院大学人間福祉学部非常勤講師）

Thinking about Human Life and Society
人間生活と社会福祉を読み解く新たな視点

1　刷　　2023 年 2 月 7 日　　[B-950]
2　刷　　2024 年 2 月14日

編著者　　茨木正志郎　（Seishirou Ibaraki）
Sam Haugh　（サム・ホー）
中野陽子　（Yoko Nakano）
西村浩子　（Hiroko Nishimura）
小林亮哉　（Ryoya Kobayashi）

発行者　　南雲　一範　Kazunori Nagumo
発行所　　株式会社　南雲堂
〒162-0801　東京都新宿区山吹町 361
NAN' UN-DO CO.,Ltd.
361 Yamabuki-cho, Shinjuku-ku, Tokyo 162-0801, Japan
振替口座：00160-0-46863
TEL：03-3268-2311(営業部：学校関係)
TEL：03-3268-2384(営業部：書店関係)
TEL：03-3268-2387(編集部)
FAX：03-3269-2486

編集者　　加藤　敦
組　版　　中西　史子
装　丁　　N スタジオ
検　印　　省略
コード　　ISBN 978-4-523-17950-4　C0082

Printed in Japan

E-mail　nanundo@post.email.ne.jp
URL　https://www.nanun-do.co.jp